Contents

Preface	vi

The Origins of Riding Theory — x

Goal-Oriented Schooling of the Horse	1
The Essence of the Training Scale	4
The Purpose of the German Riding Theory	7
Understanding Riding as a Conversation	10

Basic Elements: Balance and Aids — 16

Abilities versus Skills	17
The Ability to Maintain Balance in Rhythm	24
Balance and Rhythm	27
Balance Exercises on the Ground	30
Balance Exercises on the Horse	32
Exercises from the 6-Point Program in the Saddle	35
The Rider's Aids	42
Auxiliary Means Are Not Aids	58
Outlook: The Interplay of Aids	58
Independent Aids	59

Basics of Rider Preparation — 62

The Warm-Up	63
Warm-Up Rules	67
Types of Preparation	68
Active Regeneration—The Cool-Down Process	70
The Rider's Training Scale	71

Contents

Three Fundamental Riding Techniques   76

Flexion, Bend, and Half-Halts   77
Flexing—The Technique   81
Bending—The Technique   86
Half-Halts—The Technique   94

Learning How to Ride in Conversation   100

Functional Riding Instruction   101
The Planning Process   103
Instruction Against the Background of the Riding Theory   107
Communication in Riding Instruction   112

Eckart Meyners
Hannes Müller
Kerstin Niemann

Rider + Horse = 1

How to Achieve the Fluid Dialogue that Leads to Harmonious Performance

Trafalgar Square
North Pomfret, Vermont

First published in the United States of America in 2014 by
Trafalgar Square Books
North Pomfret, Vermont 05053

Originally published in the German language as *Reiten als Dialog* by Franckh-Kosmos Verlags-GmbH & Co. KG, Stuttgart

Copyright © 2011 Franckh-Kosmos Verlags
English translation © 2014 Trafalgar Square Books

All rights reserved. No part of this book may be reproduced, by any means, without written permission of the publisher, except by a reviewer quoting brief excerpts for a review in a magazine, newspaper, or website.

Disclaimer of Liability
The author and publisher shall have neither liability nor responsibility to any person or entity with respect to any loss or damage caused or alleged to be caused directly or indirectly by the information contained in this book. While the book is as accurate as the author can make it, there may be errors, omissions, and inaccuracies.

Trafalgar Square Books encourages the use of approved safety helmets in all equestrian sports and activities.

ISBN: 978-1-57076-705-0

Library of Congress Control Number: 2014948594

All photos by Horst Streitferdt/Kosmos, except: p. 1 by Gudrun Braun and pp. 33, 34, 35, 36 (top left), 42, and 129 by Andrea Marquardt/Kosmos

Illustrations by Cornelia Koller

Cover design by RM Didier
Interior design by eStudio Calamar/Atelier Krohmer
Index by Andrea M. Jones (www.jonesliteraryservices.com)
Typefaces: Palatino, Vista Sans

Printed in China

10 9 8 7 6 5 4 3 2 1

The Training Scale: The Familiarization Phase   124

The Significance of Familiarization	125
Rhythm in the Young Horse	125
The Rider's Three-Dimensionality	133
Suppleness	135
Contact	140
Creating Positive Tension	142

Impulsion, Straightening, and Collection   144

From Familiarization to Pushing and Carrying Power	145
Advanced Development of the Horse	145
Impulsion	148
Straightening	161
Collection	176
Bibliography	186
Index	188

PREFACE

When it was first discussed, this book project, intended to intertwine the insights of German Riding Theory with biomechanics, caused some very mixed feelings. These occurred even though it had been demonstrated that such a book was urgently needed, not just to show the link between Riding Theory as outlined in *The Principles of Riding Theory*, the official instruction manual of the German National Equestrian Federation (FN) and biomechanics in practical application, but also to capture it in writing. Undoubtedly, the practical seminars jointly given by riding instructor Hannes Müller and sports physiology and movement expert Eckart Meyners have always been a success, but to combine the insights of both areas in a book?

Furthermore, there were doubts about writing yet another book about Riding Theory since it is not new, nor is the Training Scale. Riding education cannot be reinvented so simply repackaging an old topic cannot be the goal of a book of 200 pages, into which, after all, each of the three participating authors has invested a lot of time, thought, interchange of ideas, and energy.

FN-certified riding instructor Martin Stammkötter completed his education at the German national stallion depot in Northrhine-Westphalia in Germany. Under the guidance of Johann Hinnemann, renowned dressage trainer and former assistant Olympic team coach, he then rode the national stallions in competition. Stammkötter is recipient of the "Goldenes Reitabzeichen" (a qualification level for German riders) and presented stallions up to Grand Prix level.

Preface

One argument for the book was the chosen perspective: a book that would literally link Riding Theory with biomechanics—the way the rider and horse actually *function*. The practical application shows that linking these can yield remarkable results in horse and rider within a short period of time, and facilitate riding in harmony.

Nowadays, unfortunately, the fact that not only the horse but also the rider must be educated with patience—and plenty of time—is often overlooked. The rider not only benefits from knowing how the aids are applied, but also from developing rider "feel." In riding arenas all over, you can still hear instructions like "Heels Down!," "Sit up Straight!" or "Head up!" All these are corrections that target the "external form" of the rider on the horse and mirror this statement: "Only a correct seat can enable a rider to give correct aids."

This statement is absolutely right! However, the conclusion all too often drawn from it goes off into the wrong direction: In order to learn how to ride with feel, it is never enough to sit on the horse in "perfect form" (and quite possibly stiff as a board!). For the rider, it is much more important to harmoniously go with the horse's movement, and not hinder him with her own stiffness or restrictions.

In this book, it's the way the rider *functions*—not her *form*—that will play the most important role. This means, of course, that it is important to know what a volte should look like in order to be able to ride it. It is more essential, however, to develop knowledge and feel for the requirements that horse and rider must bring to the table in order to recognize the "structure" of this curved line, and to coordinate your aids according to this structure. Basically, it does not matter whether you want to ride a volte, a serpentine, or any other kind of curved line; it is not about the individual school figures, but about overriding relationships of motion sequences in curved lines and their function in various schooling contexts.

If these mutual relationships can be recognized and the respective aids implemented with feel, the rider will be able to transfer these basic principles to all curved lines.

> **Note from the Authors**
>
> We are very glad that our book is now translated into English so the topic of exploring "riding as a dialogue" will reach lots of riders worldwide. The aim of translating complex topics into another language and to find the exact words for many definitions is ambitious because for some German technical equestrian terms there are no exact English equivalents.
>
> —Kerstin Niemann/
> Hannes Müller/Eckart Meyners

Conclusion

When you meet the requirements of *function, form* will automatically be correct. Not the other way around.

This book will *not* tell you the differences between riding a volte and a serpentine. Instead, you will learn the answers to the following questions:

Which principles are behind the worldwide recognized Training Scale?

What correlation is there between the individual areas of ability in the Training Scale (see p. 2)?

And in which basic abilities and skills (aids, techniques, lessons) must a rider be proficient in order to be able to correctly influence the horse in such a way so that the six abilities of the Training Scale can be developed?

It is our wish and goal to present the activity of riding as a conversation between human and horse in a way that is easy to understand and reproduce. The "dialogic-movement concept" developed by the

1 *Mandy Zimmer hails from Luxembourg and continues her riding education with Olympic Champion and former coach of the German national team Klaus Balkenhol. Her professional goal is to become an FN-certified assistant instructor. She has experience in showing horses up to Grand Prix level. During the photo shoot for this book, she experienced the link between biomechanics and the German Riding Theory for the first time.*

2 *The equestrian sports journalist and FN-certified Assistant Instructor Kerstin Niemann experienced problems regaining her suppleness on a horse after a riding accident.*

Dutch scientist Jan Tamboer has proven its value in practical application and in science.

The perspective of the conversational-movement concept starts from the premise that during the lesson, the rider—to the greatest extent possible—is not *passively* moved (except by the riding instructor's instruction), but rather is *actively* moving *herself*.

Transferred to practical riding applications this means mostly that a rider acts mostly independently and is goal-oriented in any given situation. In other words, the rider uses her own movement to act on a specific intent in regard to the horse in various riding situations—for example, in an indoor or outdoor arena, or on the trail.

The conversational perspective always presupposes that there is insight into the meaning of the relationship between rider, horse, and a riding situation. The rider strives for the *function*, the purpose and intent of rider and horse, not primarily their *outward appearance*. This is not about purely "mechanically" ridden sequences, but in this model of rider and horse movement, muscular, nerve, and mental processes are of significant importance in that they are partial conditions for function.

For decades, we have all been working with the education of horses and riders, and while working on this book, we were able to gain many new insights. Familiar topics were revived, seemingly boring theory suddenly became exciting again, and many questions were discussed in all-night sessions. In the end, this led to the certainty: This book is necessary, since the connection between Riding Theory and biomechanics has been the missing link. Today, it is not enough for trainers and riding instructors just to master Riding Theory in order to recognize the underlying reasons for horse and rider problems. Instead, it is necessary for Riding Theory and biomechanics to form one *unit* and, against this backdrop, for riding instruction to be even more supportive.

We hope that we can present you the link between rider and horse movement in a way that makes it transparently clear. After all, the feeling of being in a conversation with your horse, *of becoming one with him,* is what makes riding so unique.

Eckart Meyners, Hannes Müller, Kerstin Niemann

The successful dressage rider and FN-certified Assistant Instructor Helen Langehanenberg completed her apprenticeship with Ingrid Klimke, winner of team gold medals in eventing in Beijing, 2008, and London, 2012, and daughter of the late Dr. Reiner Klimke. Helen won the team silver medal in dressage at the 2012 Olympics, and the team gold and individual silver medals at the 2014 World Equestrian Games in Normandy, France.

The Origins of Riding Theory

Goal-Oriented Schooling of the Horse

The preoccupation with schooling the horse has a long tradition. For many centuries, however, there had not been a generally recognized theory: The horse's schooling was always guided by his designated use. A workhorse, for instance, was a valuable economic asset in agriculture and forestry; he had to be strong and possess "pulling power." For military use the horse had to possess good stamina—among other qualities—in order to be fast and agile during combat.

In the riding schools, on the other hand, it was all about riding culture, beauty, elegance, and purity of the horse. It was in this area of riding where the first writings or theories regarding the schooling of the horse were developed. Various great riding masters like Xenophon, de la Guériniére, and the Duke of Newcastle put their thoughts, deliberations, and experiences on paper and called them a "riding system" or a "riding theory." Throughout the centuries, these existing writings continued to be supplemented and developed.

Army Regulation from 1912

From collected works such as those by Xenophon, Francois Robichon de la Guériniére and Antoine de Pluvinel, the hippologist Gustav Steinbrecht, born in 1808, developed his thoughts that were first edited, completed, and published by his student Paul Plinzner under the title *The Gymnasium of the Horse*. But only through the revision and comments from Colonel Hans von Heydebreck has this work gained

The Army Regulations from 1912, in German called Heeresdienstvorschrift *and abbreviated as HDV 12, was developed from the collected works of various hippologists (among others,* The Gymnasium of the Horse*). This compilation of specialized riding knowledge served as the basis for today's* The Principles of Riding and Driving, *the official instruction manual of the German National Equestrian Federation (FN).*

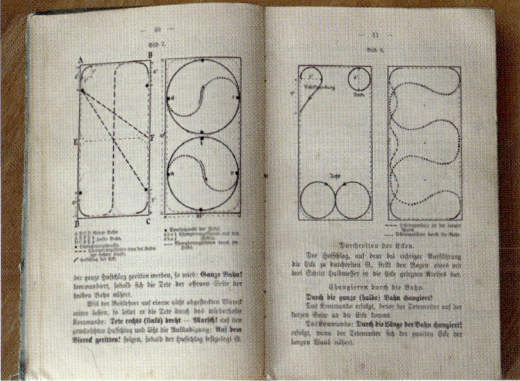

The Origins of Riding Theory

To this date, this statue embodies the classical riding education: The bronze of the dressage rider Baron Carl Friedrich von Langen on Draufgänger, champion at the 1928 Olympic Games (sculpture in the horse museum, Verden).

the significance it has today. It served as the basis for the contents that were later developed into the Army Regulation of 1912 (abbreviated as *HDV 12*), that, in turn, were the basis for today's *Principles of Riding and Driving* of the German National Equestrian Federation (FN).

The necessity for the *HDV 12* arose from the situation at the time. In previous centuries, the riding horse had mainly been used for military purposes; it became the basis for the creation of a comprehensive set of regulations for the education of the *military* horse.

The goal of these regulations was to create a type of instruction manual that did the nature of the horse justice and met the requirements of his life as a military horse. The rules that today we call the Riding Theory—also known as the Guidelines of the German National Equestrian Federation (FN)—are based upon this set of regulations, which was developed over the course of centuries.

At its core is a globally recognized schooling principal, called the "Training Scale." Its six central abilities, Rhythm, Suppleness, Contact and Acceptance of the Bit, Impulsion, Straightening, and Collection are abilities a horse must develop during his schooling. The success of this schooling principle was already demonstrated during the first zenith of equine sports during the 1930s, as well as the global recognition of the German Riding Theory, including the Training Scale.

The Horse as Partner in Sports and Recreational Activity

Once military use of the horse became obsolete and agriculture became mechanized, use of the horse altered dramatically. Horse breeding of the past had focused on agriculture—during the 1950s, for example, the German national stallion depot in North Rhine-Westphalia had about 150 draft horse stallions and only about 50 Warmblood stallions, while today the ratio is almost the opposite—a new area of use for the horse developed after World War II, and that was equestrian sport.

Today, the majority of all horses in most countries are either used for performance sports or recreational riding. Many riders don't want to spend time or effort on developing good cooperation between themselves and their horse; they don't find it necessary or appropriate.

While in the past horses were predominantly used for military service and agriculture, today the horse is mainly used for pleasure riding and performance sports.

However, there is no "light version" of riding. Without basic knowledge regarding the biomechanics of rider and horse, you cannot learn a complex athletic activity such as riding. For ethical reasons, therefore, the responsible rider is obligated to school herself and the horse in her care according to the Training Scale.

The Essence of the Training Scale

The schooling of the horse has basically four fundamental goals:

- Proper riding is animal welfare in action.
- Schooling is the best accident prevention.
- Only the proficient rider can enjoy riding.
- Sustainable improvement in performance is only possible with schooling that does the nature of the horse justice.

Riding is a complex sport since the goal is to bring two moving creatures into a harmonious dialogue. This is impossible without knowledge of the Riding Theory and biomechanics.

The essence of the Training Scale is defined by the fact that none of the six abilities—Rhythm, Suppleness, Contact and Acceptance of the Bit, Impulsion, Straightening, and Collection—should be viewed as an isolated topic. It is not possible to exchange the sequence of this hierarchical system of abilities, since they are scaled from the elementary to the most difficult.

For example: Rhythm and Suppleness, even under the rider, are fundamental elementary abilities of the horse. Only when the horse has these can he develop more complex abilities under the rider, such as *driving power* or *carrying power*.

Conclusion: The Training Scale has a complex structure with several functions:

Short-Term: It structures a riding lesson or session.

Long-term: It serves as a sustainable, total guideline for schooling.

It has a control function over the success of schooling work by making it possible to analyze schooling problems and solutions.

It takes several levels of conversation for rider and horse to ultimately merge as "one." The exchanges must not only happen between horse and rider, but also between rider and instructor.

Misinterpretations of the Training Scale

- There is an assumption that the Training Scale is only relevant to the sport of dressage but this is not correct. The principles of the Training Scale apply to horses in all disciplines, whether in the performance sports—dressage, jumping, and driving—or recreational riding.
- Within the Riding Theory, there is special terminology that a rider must know, understand, and be able to apply. Often, however, the

The goal of schooling is to develop the horse according to his natural predisposition. Nature, so to speak, predefines the horse's schooling path. Therefore, it can be said that schooling the horse is "copying from nature."

meanings of these specialized terms are derived from colloquial language, which does not reflect the complexity of the overall situations.
- Due to its ascending hierarchical structure, many view the Training Scale as a rigid system that restricts rider and horse. They overlook the fact that there is a high degree of variability within individual areas of ability in terms of a multifaceted and varied education, which means many different lessons can be used in order to achieve the same goal (through a *systematic* approach, rather than a *schematic* approach).
- The Training Scale is seemingly "only" concerned with the basic schooling of the horse. A horse schooled to Second Level has actually gone through all six areas of ability of the Scale during his basic training. You might be confused by the fact that as the performance requirements increase, no new areas of ability are added. Instead, the *quality* of ability increases until maximum performance of an individual horse has been reached.

> **Natural Movements**
> The horse's movements under the rider are derived from nature.

To illustrate, here is an example that relates to the development of the length of stride in the trot: The basis is the rhythmic working trot from which lengthening of the strides is developed. From this increased impulsion, the horse is brought back to beginning collection. The rider verifies this, in turn, by extending the pace, meaning she is riding the medium trot. With an increasing schooling level, the horse can be brought back to an improved collection in the medium trot, which, in turn, leads to the extended trot by means of improved extension.

This basic principle of explaining lessons and exercises from elementary to the complex system from the bottom up will continue to be used during the following chapters in this book.

The Purpose of the German Riding Theory

Riding is often viewed—especially by non-riders—as an activity in which the horse is forced to perform. To many people, it is not evident how this works and how the interplay between rider and horse takes place.

Watching sophisticated exercises such as piaffe or watching a horse tackle a five-foot obstacle—whether during training or in a high-class

The Origins of Riding Theory

During interaction with other members of the herd, horses in the pasture show all movements that can later be developed under saddle. The display behavior of stallions, for example, is similar to the movements of piaffe and passage as required in high-level dressage tests.

dressage or jumping show—often leads to a lack of understanding in the uninitiated spectator: Why is the horse asked to perform such movements? Dressage movements such as passage or piaffe are seen as artificial ("drilled horses"), and jumping over high obstacles is viewed as a violation of the horse. Eventing competition, where horses must tackle the most difficult cross-country obstacles, is often viewed negatively, as well.

All these riding situations are only possible because horses naturally possess the abilities needed. It would be impossible to elicit these behaviors from the horse—no matter how sophisticated the Riding Theory—if he did not already possess the inner willingness and the genuine movement repertoire.

In this context, it is important to mention that the horse does not need a Riding Theory since he is inherently capable of all the movements needed.

Passage and *piaffe* are natural movements: Watch how a stallion behaves when he approaches a mare in heat. You can see how expressively he presents himself to the mare with movements that are similar to passage and piaffe. And horses are also naturally able to clear obstacles by jumping.

The difference between movements in his natural environment and movements required in today's sports environment (many of which are "artificial"), is that when mounted, the rider destroys the horse's natural way of moving, which thus needs to be "rebuilt" for riding.

It was for this purpose that today's so-called classical riding theory was developed over the course of centuries. Originally, this experienced-based theory was developed by numerous horse trainers and riding instructors into a precise and coherent schooling system for horses (and riders), and it incorporates modern, horse-related, scientific findings.

All this is summarized in Volumes 1 and 2 of the *Principles of Riding and Driving* of the German National Equestrian Federation (FN). The Training Scale included in these principles is the best biomechanics theory for the horse. As already mentioned, it was developed from the *HDV 12*, which focused on the schooling of the horse (see p. 2). A prerequisite for this was that the rider had a thorough education. Today, however, this fact has largely been forgotten.

> **Riding and Kinematics**
> The aim of this book is to help you as a rider understand how your body works and how your body needs to correspond with the natural movements of the horse. Only when the rider has learned to establish a link between the act of riding and the theory of motion can the horse move correctly under the rider and rider and horse can become one.

The Rider in the Course of Time

Just as horses today no longer primarily move in a natural way, neither do riders. In today's affluent society, human beings have lost the ability to sensibly manage their own body. The reasons: They generally move too little and when they do, there is not enough variety. This results in physical and mental deficits, as well as coordination issues.

It has led to substantial deficits in the way the human interacts with the horse. The horse's natural needs and the human's understanding of these should be a fundamental element of the rider's education: Only a rider who thoroughly understands the horse is able to school a horse according to his nature.

Furthermore, the rider's education must include learning how to manage her own body in order to gain the abilities and skills necessary to naturally handle her own movement—and the movement of the horse.

Only by restoring the naturalness of rider and horse is it possible for joint endeavors, whether in the area of performance sports or pleasure riding, to be performed in a relatively relaxed manner and, therefore, become the equivalent of a harmonious conversation.

Understanding Riding as a Conversation

In order for the horse to rediscover his natural way of going when under the rider, the rider must develop a specific understanding of riding itself. Riding in this sense must not be a process guided by purely *mechanical* principles (*form* before *function*.) If that were the case, only the *bodies* of the two partners would be of importance. But, as we understand it, riding follows the perspective that it is only possible to achieve harmony between human and horse when you know the process between them must be a *conversation*.

The walk is the only basic gait without impulsion. People often do not recognize how difficult it is to not *disturb the horse in this gait. He needs his "balancing rod," the neck, in order to be able to maintain rhythm in the walk.*

So what does "riding in conversation" actually mean?

Each rider moves differently on her horse, even though the rider is expected to maintain the so-called correct seat according to the Riding Theory during lessons.

But there is no such thing as a proper or correct seat for everyone, since each rider is an individual being with her own characteristic conditions—on a physical, intellectual, and mental level.

This explains why the rider's coordination with the horse is always "unfinished process" because it is constantly changing.

From sports science we know that there is only one optimal "movement solution" (i.e. function) for each human and each motion pattern. When riding, therefore, we need to determine these individual movement solutions for each horse-and-rider combination.

The cooperation of human and horse should be in harmony and function as a conversation between two beings that are understanding and responsive to one another.

When you understand riding as a conversation, you presuppose that both partners are actively participating in the creation of this dialogue. The rider must not force the horse into a "form" or "shape" just as she should not conform with rigid, formal seat specifications for herself.

As a rider, you should follow this maxim:

"When working with a horse in any way, try to feel how you influence the horse and what he then wants from you. If you, at first, give in to his will, he will later give in to yours." (Tholey, 1987, page 101).

You can clearly see the complex, three-dimensional motion patterns in the horse's back and the rider's pelvis when viewing horse and rider from behind in the trot. The rider, following the movement of the horse's back, needs to be able to move her pelvis to the right and left, up and down, as well as back and forth.

The Origins of Riding Theory

The rider emits signals through her body language that the horse understands, and he reacts to her driving aids by pushing off nicely with his hind limbs.

    Riding in this sense, means, therefore, that the rider sends messages by means of her body language, that is, via the various aids, which the horse must understand and reply to.

    A distinctive feature of this sport is that the back of the horse and the rider's pelvis move in three dimensions and must harmonize in this movement (forward and back, right to left, up and down). This feature is also the reason for riding-specific problems.

Understanding Riding as a Conversation

A Developmental Edge

Conversational communication is only successful when one of the two partners has a "developmental edge." When the rider is competent—in terms of emotional, cognitive, technical, and "feel" competence—she will be able to recognize through her body what the horse accepts and what he does not, in order to be able to act and react in a flexible and responsive manner. If the horse reacts with uncertainty, the rider must be able to change her aids in a way so that he can accept and implement them (this demonstrates flexibility on the part of the rider according to the horse's situation). Both partners' language "systems" must therefore adapt to each other during the conversation: They must get to the same "language level."

The same applies to the experienced horse that is able to "recall" the desired riding movements even when an inexperienced rider transfers her aids to him in an insecurely coordinated fashion.

The goal for both beings is to learn to "listen" to their own inner voice and to their partner in order to understand themselves and the other being.

Conversation Equals Harmonious Interaction

The goal is for each partner, meaning rider and horse, to continue to grow more and more distinctly into a harmonious unit for longer periods of time.

From this perspective, you cannot look at rider and horse merely as bodies that move in dressage or jumping, for example, but instead as two independent, individual beings that, together, negotiate a common task. In other words, the horse is not a piece of exercise equipment.

The rider as well as the horse has a specific personality that must be recognized and combined into a harmonious overall picture.

In conversation, each being can alternately behave in a dominant, then more compliant manner depending on the situation. It is important to keep focusing on these individual types of interaction rather than on the motion patterns being ridden, which can only be seen by an observer. When we speak of riding, we must not only observe and judge the outer appearance of a horse and rider but realize that only when we are also able to capture an *"inner image,"* that is a *feel for the*

From the position and movement of his ears and his body posture (low poll), the horse in the top photo is showing that the dialogue between rider and horse has become disrupted and the rider is not going with the horse's movement.
The horse's ears in the bottom photo indicate that there is a good conversation going on between rider and horse. One ear is pointing toward the rider while the other is going toward the horse's direction of movement.

A Developmental Edge

The inexperienced rider should ride a schooled horse while the schooled rider should ride an inexperienced horse.

In order to develop a feel for the movement, a young rider must receive a varied education. Besides riding dressage, she should also jump and go for pleasure rides even when things are not perfect from the get-go.

movement of the rider, can we can gain a complete impression of the pair's presentation.

We must not only understand the rider's engagement with the horse as a conversation, but also the way in which the rider carries on a dialogue with herself. Her motion patterns should make it clear that she is not just riding in a "mechanical" fashion but that her aids and the horse's responses are a *functional* part of achieving specific tasks or goals.

The rider's goal must be to merge with the horse in such a way so that an observer can recognize there is unity between the motion (i.e. movement harmony) of both beings.

Harmony means that the horse's movements are being transferred to the rider and the rider's movements are transferred to the horse in such a way that results in joint movement flow. This type of movement flow is present when there are no noticeable awkward sequences, and no jerky, partial movements. Instead, there is a coordinated, conversational interaction of all movement by both beings.

The terms "dialogue" or "conversation" and "harmony" also refer to the interaction between the instructor and the horse-and-rider pair. It is also in this context that the mutuality of the communication processes should be visible. This means that riding lessons should not merely follow an instructional schematic, but must—as much as possible—be conducted with mutually developed tasks (see p. 101).

Soft, flowing movement indicates there is a good conversation going on between rider and horse.

Summary

- For many centuries, there was no generally recognized riding theory, in spite of the fact that many riding masters focused on the schooling of the horse.
- At the beginning of the 20th century, the Army Regulations of 1912 (HDV 12) was created. Its contents are largely reflected in today's *Principles of Riding and Driving*.
- There has been a significant change in the way we use the horse. Today, most horses are kept as a partner for sport and recreational activities.
- The schooling of the horse has four fundamental goals: maintaining the horse's health (animal welfare), accident prevention, enjoyment, and improvement in performance. These goals can be sustainably achieved by the application of the Training Scale.
- The Training Scale is a system that serves as an aid for schooling a horse according to his individual nature. Many riders, however, find it too complicated.

Basic Elements: Balance and Aids

Abilities versus Skills

Before we can elaborate on balance, rhythm, and aids in the following chapters, we must more closely examine the correlation between ability and skill from the perspective of biomechanics. In biomechanics, movement analysis differentiates between an *interior* and *exterior* view. The mechanics of *internal* movement are hard to observe so movement can only be explored by means of *externally* visible features. In this context, ability is an aspect of the interior view, while skill is an aspect of the exterior view.

Ability

Biomechanics experts speak of *ability* in terms of how it can be applied to various athletic activities and how it constitutes a basic prerequisite for movement.

Abilities do not strictly apply to one type of sport (riding, soccer, etc.) or a movement technique (javelin throw, high jump, etc.), but are applicable across various types of sports and techniques.

In this context, we differentiate between coordinative and conditional ability. Coordinative ability is information-oriented, while conditional ability is energy-oriented.

A Harmonious Conversation
Only a rider who possesses coordinative and conditional abilities can enter into harmonious conversation with the horse.

coordinative abilities = information-oriented	conditional abilities = energy-oriented
balance rhythm responsiveness visual orientation situational adaptability kinesthetic differentiation (ability to adjust muscular tension/force needed to produce a desired result) coupling capability (ability to interact with another)	speed, how quickly you can reach certain speeds, how long you can maintain them strength, how quickly you can summon strength, how long you can maintain it endurance, and your ability to maintain speed and strength over time

In order to produce harmonious motion patterns, the rider must be supple from the head (1), over the shoulders (2) and the pelvis (3), to the feet (4). Various exercises in the saddle can contribute to this suppleness.

Information-oriented means that this ability depends on the information received by the senses: ears, eyes, skin, sense of movement, and sense of balance in the inner ear. Among other things, *coordinative* ability includes the ability to maintain balance and rhythm; the ability to react and to orient yourself by means of visual clues; the ability to adapt to changing situations; the ability to differentiate kinesthetically; and the "coupling" ability.

Energy-oriented ability is a *conditional* ability such as speed, strength, and endurance.

Skills

In sports, the external aspect of movement (exterior view) becomes visible in the form of skill. Skills in the sport of riding are techniques such as the rein back, lateral movements, and half-pirouettes in the walk. In order to be able to perform these riding skills, the rider must first master the interplay of the weight, leg, and rein aids, which are needed to perform the three fundamental riding techniques: *flexing*, *bending*, and *half-halt* (see p. 77). With these three riding techniques, the rider will be able to achieve any gymnasticizing effects in the horse.

Abilities and Skills in Riding

Balance and rhythm are of fundamental significance for the rider's level of coordination. A rider's motion patterns can only be in rhythm when she is balanced. Every rhythm fault is a balance fault. A rider who is not in balance and rhythm has to pay so much attention to herself that she cannot control her aids, her technique, and, thus, her riding skills: She works against the horse and is unable to form a harmonious unit with him.

The three most important rider aids are weight, leg, and rein aids. None of these aids is applied in isolation; they are always applied in correlation with another. Weight and leg aids produce energy that flows through the horse's body to his mouth.

The rider's body is like a ship's mast. Any change in position in any individual body part affects the body's position as a whole.

The Ability to Maintain Balance

The *emotional* and *physical* balance of any human being correlate to one another: Emotional imbalances cause physical imbalances, and vice-versa. The rider is "thrown out of kilter," and her body no longer functions optimally.

One model that has proven effective in illustrating the way the human body works in this context is the "ship's mast." The key idea behind this model is that any change of position in any body part immediately results in changes to the entire system.

Human fear, for instance, is expressed by pulling up the shoulders, or tilting them forward or to the side. These changes to the shoulders' position automatically affect the body's entire "rigging" system. As a result, the body shifts, not only in the sternum area, but also in the hips, knees, and even all the way into the feet.

When interpreting the "ship's mast" model, we must consider that the "mast" of the human body—the spinal column—is not stable, but unstable. Therefore, we cannot compare the spinal column with a stable ship's mast, but must take into account that the spine is malleable. So whenever there is emotional stress already tearing at muscular balance, problems with natural imbalance will be even more exaggerated.

Almost all people in our society do not move enough, resulting in postural and movement dysfunction. This applies to riders just as it does to other athletes. Almost every rider has muscular imbalances that are the cause for rider weaknesses or faults.

One-sided stresses of modern life, incorrect weight-bearing, overstressing, and lack of—or incorrect—gymnasticizing, all lead to continued shortening of muscles that, by nature, are already prone to shortening.

It is necessary, therefore, to compensate for this shortening by targeting "lengthening," that is, stretching, among other things. Inactivity, unused muscle groups, and incorrect gymnasticizing lead to

Strengthening Exercises

1 *Back musculature*   **2** *Back musculature*

3 *Straight abdominal muscles*   **4** *Transverse abdominal muscles*

5 + 6 *Entire back of the rider*

7 *Entire front of the rider*

Strengthening Exercises

These exercises can compensate for the rider's movement deficits, benefitting her seat on the horse. They can be performed in a slow, dynamic fashion. In this case, it is necessary to do 8 to 12 repetitions (a set). Depending on the rider's fitness, she can perform several sets.

These same exercises, however, can also each be performed in a static fashion. In this case, the end position should be held for 10 seconds. It can also be repeated with a break of 15 to 20 seconds between each repetition.

increased weakening of muscles that already tend to be weak. Every rider should become aware of these interconnections and ensure—by practicing the respective exercises—that these muscles are deliberately strengthened (revitalized) in order to prevent the imbalance from becoming even greater. This is best done before mounting!

Balance as a Fundamental Sensory Ability

Balance is a human ability very closely connected to all senses. Vestibular disorders (vertigo) have a negative effect on senses (Ayres/Robins). A rider not in balance automatically has problems in applying her senses to the task of learning skills—riding techniques, aids.

When the rider needs to continuously pay attention to her balance, her eyes are automatically inhibited from taking in information. For example, she can't apply her aids in a manner that will enable her to perform the dressage movements at their respective markers. The show jumper will consequently always have problems with distances before a jump.

Varying, even unusual, seat positions can help a rider find her individual balance in the saddle.

What is the Definition of Balance?

Depending on the situation that needs to be coped with, we differentiate between standing balance, translocational balance, rotational balance, and unsupported balance.

In the human, the vestibular and kinesthetic systems are responsible for coping with balance.

The vestibular sensory organ is located in the inner ear, which is filled with liquid and contains an arrangement of highly sensitive little hairs with crystals that transmit any positional changes to the brain. Inside the ear, there are three additional systems (the sacculus, utriculus, semicircular canals) that are responsible for transmitting forward, backward, up and down, and rotating movement. Among others, the vestibular system works in unison with sensory organs such as the eye and ear and signals the respective differences in body position in motion patterns to the brain, so that these differences can be compensated for.

It is important that the head is not tilted too far forward, too far back, or carried while tilted sideways. In these positions, the information intake in the inner ear is distorted and the compensation control does not occur appropriately, according to the situation.

The kinesthetic system receives information from receptors at joints, tendons, and muscles—so-called "proprioceptors." These register position changes in the body faster than any receptors of the other senses (eye, ear, skin). Imbalances are compensated for by means of minute muscle activity, which keeps the human in balance.

The proprioceptors are connected to all other receptors and, in themselves, form a complete functioning unit. They are able to register and compensate disturbances of equilibrium so quickly that an onlooker would not even notice that the person had lost her balance.

Prerequisites for obtaining a high sensibility of the vestibular and kinesthetic systems (analysts) are a multitude of comprehensive movements by the human. Only by continuously stimulating (i.e. training) both systems will these be best educated and maintain their performance and transmission ability.

Cross-coordination exercises are especially helpful for the rider's brain and body, and when they are performed while jumping, they help to support the unsupported balance.

The Human's Ability to Maintain Balance

Every human acquires *standing* balance during the course of her natural growth. This is the basis for a healthy development of her personality, for example, self-confidence and personal identity.

Translocational balance is an ability a rider possesses to enable balance on the horse not while walking, but rather while sitting. The rider must possess this ability to a great extent in order to ride without problems.

Rotational balance means the ability to pivot around one's own center without having to perform large movements with arms and hands in order to compensate.

Unsupported balance is the human's ability to lift up off the ground, spiral straight up into the air, then land securely. In the process, the human must not abandon the straight body posture (longitudinal axis) during landing.

You Cannot Learn Movement Without Balance

Balance is one of several coordinative abilities that form the basis for learning a movement. We can define balance as the most important ability. A person who is struggling for balance cannot pay attention to other movement requirements and she is, therefore, limited as far as learning movement is concerned.

Right from the start of a riding education, the rider faces many detailed movements and skill requirements (e.g. coordination of aids) within her own body and in contact with the horse. In the course of education, these requirements continue to increase. Consequently, the rider with an impaired sense of balance will have great difficulty coordinating her own body and cooperating with the horse.

From the perspective of sports education, coordination means the muscular interaction of all individual movements within the rider, that is, a harmonious attunement of the rider's individual body parts that are also coordinated with the horse's movement (total coordination of rider and horse, see *Rider Fitness: Body & Brain* by Eckart Meyners, 2011).

The Ability to Maintain Balance in Rhythm

The ability to maintain balance in rhythm has a reciprocal relationship, which means that a rider can only move in rhythm when she is in complete emotional, muscular, vestibular, and kinesthetic balance.

A lack of balance can cause rhythm irregularities. Each time rhythm is upset it is a sign that the rider is not in balance.

As it relates to muscular imbalance, we must highlight that a rhythm issue can also arise as a result of physical restrictions.

In these situations, an instructor must figure out whether the rider's weakness is a result of lack of balance or muscular imbalances.

Rhythm is defined as the structure of a movement in terms of time, space, and dynamics. It is about the recurrence of contraction and relaxation movement in the rider overall, or in partial movement.

Furthermore, rhythm can be defined as *object* rhythm and *subject* rhythm. The horse provides the rider with *object* rhythm. Due to his size, musculature, head/neck leverage as it relates to the back, and

---

What Is Influence?

First of all, the rider must adjust herself to the horse's movement. Only by "melting into" the horse is it possible to positively influence the horse's movement by means of weight, leg, and rein aids. This is called "influence."

temperament, the *young* horse can only move in his natural rhythm: He is not yet able to move according to the requirements of the Training Scale.

So, in order to interact in harmony with the horse, the rider must adjust to this object rhythm.

Only when the rider is able to move in identical rhythm with the horse will she be able to change the horse's rhythm through her own body. Then the horse will be able to move his best according to the

In order for the horse to recover his natural balance under the rider's weight, it is essential that the rider herself is in balance and can align herself to the horse's rhythm.

Due to the differences in rhythm, each gait presents a distinct challenge to the rider: The walk is a four-beat, the trot a two-beat, and the canter a three-beat gait. A rider must learn to quickly adjust to the changing motion sequences during transitions.

Riding Theory. In riding terminology, this subjective change is called "influence."

Example: It is easy to observe the coordinated interaction between horse and rider when the rider is posting the trot. An external indication of optimal rhythm is a steady, soft, and harmonious flow of movement in the transitions and repetitions, also the horse's tempo and rhythm.

Only when the rider is in balance as well as in rhythm is it possible for her to apply her skills (techniques and aids) since she can adjust to the horse and feel when she should use which aid. Both of their rhythms merge—they "amalgamate." (Meinel/Schnabel, 2007).

This creates a basis for being able to "feel" yourself into the horse's movement, and to conduct a conversation with the horse that is as free from interference as possible, since coordinative abilities and skills are the language that riders use to communicate. Therefore, on your part, there will be need to be an ongoing process of listening to the horse (through ability), and being effective (through skill). (See Meyners 2009).

Balance and Rhythm

It is essential for the rider to bring a well-developed feeling for balance and rhythm to the table in order to first, follow the horse's movement, and later, influence this movement positively.

The rider's influence affects three fundamentals: the horse's gait, direction of movement, and posture.

Since the rider is the one who removes the horse from his original environment and gets him out of balance by sitting on his back, it's always the rider's primary goal to restore the horse's natural balance (see p. 125).

This is the theme that is the "golden thread" throughout the entire schooling of the horse: In spite of the additional load presented by the rider's weight, the horse must maintain his balance.

In this context, it makes no difference whether we are talking about a young, inexperienced horse or an already schooled horse—that is, a horse unfamiliar with rider weight and aids, or one that already knows about aids and the rider's influence. Not only at the beginning of schooling, but also at the beginning of each riding session, the main concern is that rider and horse can align themselves and find their natural rhythm during movement.

When a beginner starts her riding education, it makes little sense to confront her with the fact that she should ride her horse through the poll, give a correct canter aid, or flex and bend him to the inside during turns. This simply overwhelms her since she has not yet developed sufficient coordination. Instead, her influence can only be developed after she has learned to maintain balance and rhythm on a moving horse in all the gaits.

So it is all about permitting the rider to be moved by the horse. Later, she will consciously influence the horse.

This mutual attunement, this harmonizing between rider and horse, should be the beginning of each riding session and always the goal of schooling at every level.

Finding the Rhythm—Every Day

Essentially, each session starts the same way: Rider and horse find their rhythm and synchronize it. Only then can harmonious conversation occur.

What Are the Effects of Aids?

We have already established that the rider uses aids to influence gait, posture, and tempo. A prerequisite for applying the aids in the three basic gaits of walk, trot, and canter is the rider's ability to maintain rhythm during movement: This means that the rider must first of all "listen" then respond, and become attuned to the various rhythms of the different gaits. She must follow the horse's rhythm and beat. Only when she is able to do this, can she change the rhythm/beat that the horse offers. The walk is the gait that is most prone to rhythm "interference" since it does not have a suspension phase. In the gaits that do have a suspension phase, the rider can regulate and influence the horse's rhythm by gently tilting her pelvis.

The rider can also actively change the horse's posture. Depending to what extent she applies the driving aids then retains these aids in turn with her rein aids, she can bring the horse into various frames (shape): By lengthening the rein, the horse will open his throatlatch and the rider can achieve the maximum extension posture (long and low) by letting the horse "chew" the reins out of her hands. And, when the rider gently and skillfully retains the driving impulse with her hands, the horse will increasingly elevate his neck and poll (images above).

The rider applies the exact same principle when changing the tempo of a gait. In the photo at top right, the rider wants to increase collection in his horse, meaning he wants to get the horse to shorten his canter strides. The horse assumes a more elevated posture. If the rider lets his driving impulse go "through" more, as shown in the photo on the right, the magnitude of horse's movement changes and he covers more ground with his canter stride.

Balance Exercises on the Ground

Here are a few exercises as examples. There are many other useful exercises that you can find in Eckart Meyners' book *Rider Fitness: Body & Brain*.

Exercises in motion
- Walking with positional changes: on the heels (1), on the ball of the foot (2), on the outer edge (3), on the inner edge (4).
- Jumping on one leg (5).
- High-knee skips (skipping run) while twisting the hip area (6-8).

Balance Exercises on the Ground

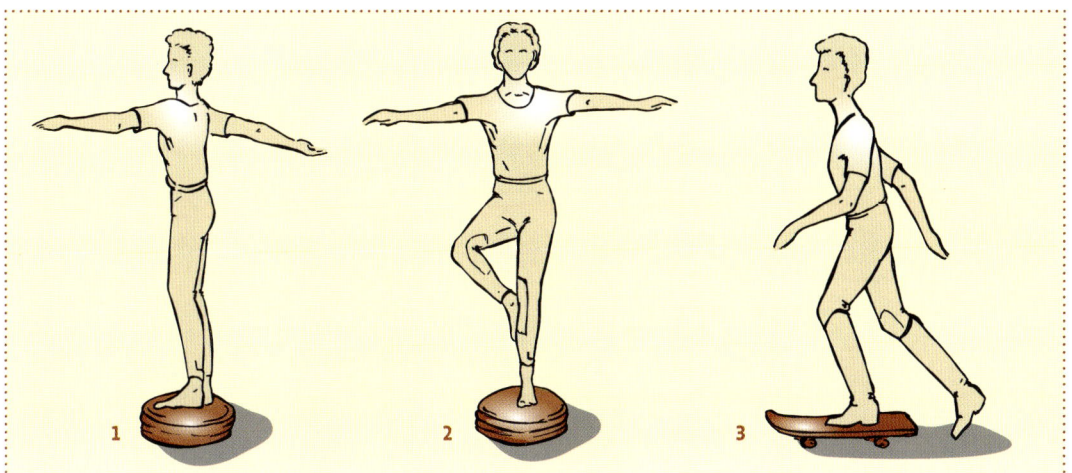

Exercises on a Balance Trainer
- Stand on both feet while turning the upper body (1).
- Stand on one leg, then on the outer edge, the inner edge, the heel, and the ball of the foot (2).

Exercises on Mobile Equipment
- Keeping your balance on a skateboard (3).

Exercises with a Stability Ball
- Crouching down, then getting back up (4).
- Lying on the ball on your stomach while stretching the body (5).

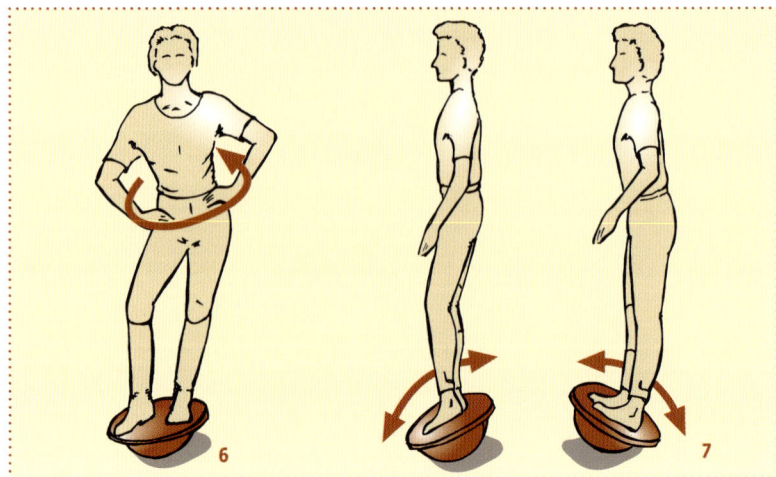

Exercises with a Bosu® Balance Trainer
- Step on to the Bosu then rotate the hip (6).
- Shift the balance point forward and back (7). It is also beneficial to shift the weight from right to left.

Balance Exercises on the Horse

Seat Exercises on the Longe

The assumption that seat exercises performed on the longe line without reins and stirrups improve the seat cannot be confirmed from the perspective of exercise science. According to the exercise science approach of Functional Theory (Göhner), changes in motion sequences in humans can only occur if—in regard to position and energy—the same processes occur as in the alternate situation as in the original situation. This is not the case when the rider does not hold the reins or rides without stirrups.

However, the positive effect of seat exercises on the longe line makes them an integral part of riding instruction: When riding without stirrups without assuming any position or form, the rider can learn that the horse helps her become more flexible. The rider is able to focus on being "moved" by the horse. Later, this "improvement" often has a positive effect on learning the so-called "proper" seat.

> **Seat Exercises**
> Conventional seat exercises on the longe line should be replaced by exercises of riding in different seat positions. Accomplishing a variety of tasks enables the rider to develop a more flexible seat.

Unfortunately, during conventional seat exercises on the longe line, students are often rigidly pressed into a "position": They are supposed to sit erect and lengthen the leg, among other things. In doing so, there is no consideration of the fact that these stretches will make the rider all the more stiff and rigid: This exaggerated lengthening of the leg can block the pelvis.

During seat exercises on the longe line without reins or stirrups, the rider should not be asked to hold her arms in a "correct" manner as if she were actually holding the reins, nor to pull up her toes. When the hands are used like this, the rider is mostly using muscles that she would not use when riding with reins.

Pulling up the toes also causes tension in the entire leg and the hip, and the rider's seat becomes unstable. Soft contact with the stirrups helps to bring heel and toes into their natural position but artificially pulling up the toes (and pushing the heels down) without stirrups just blocks the leg. So, when riding without stirrups, you should hold the legs in a natural, relaxed position.

Contrasting Exercises on the Longe Line

Contrasting exercises (using different seat positions) enable the rider to use *feel* to find out what her optimal seat position is at the time. Contrast exercises can be performed in the walk, trot, and canter.

What Creates Stiffness
Pulling up the toes or pushing the heels down while riding without stirrups (as is often practiced) not only causes stiffness in the rider's entire leg, but also in the hip. Try it yourself: Sit on a saddle without stirrups, pull your toes up and let them down again. While doing so, place your hands underneath your seat bones (ischial tuberosities) in order to feel tension and relaxation.

Contrast exercises (assuming various seat positions) produce impulses in the brain that lead to "self organization." These enable the brain to signal the optimal seat position to the rider.

During these exercises, the rider assumes extreme positions in the saddle. She sits in the saddle in the walk, trot, and canter and slides as far as she can to the left or to the right without losing her balance. She bends her upper body as far forward and back as possible. Due to the extreme strain caused by these positions, afterward she will have an easier time finding her optimal posture: Her body is grateful for once again being able to sit according to her natural physique. Similar exercises can be performed in the two-point seat in the walk, trot, and canter.

"Monkey Position" on the Longe Line

Assuming the monkey position (two-point seat with normal posture) with the head pulled up and slightly backward (in order to free the occipital joint) leads to an elastic and balanced seat within a relatively short period of time, since this position provides the best condition for all joints in the body. Movement from the head to the feet is transferred more fluidly so that a stiff rider becomes more flexible. The seat becomes cohesive, and more coordinated.

The "monkey position" on the longe line leads to more fluid movement throughout the entire body of the rider.

Exercises from the 6-Point Program in the Saddle

The Application of the 6-Point Program on the Longe Line

Exercises on the longe line should only be performed by balanced riders. Inexperienced riders tend to clamp with their legs when riding continuously on a circle since they attempt to struggle against the centrifugal force. It is also essential to have a suitable, balanced horse available.

When performing seat exercises on the longe, you can execute most of the exercises of the 6-Point Program (more about this in *Rider Fitness: Body & Brain* by Eckart Meyners) without any problems in order to best prepare on the horse for the riding tasks that lie ahead.

The rider executes the suggested exercises on the horse in all three basic gaits: walk, trot, and canter. Afterward, she makes herself aware of how her body feels, and which changes have taken place. This is how the rider is sensitized to the inner processes of her movements.

Exercises from the 6-Point Program in the Saddle

On the following pages, you will find some examples of exercises from the 6-Point Program, which shows exercises for the six essential junctions in the rider, through which the rider's seat and her feel for movement can be improved within a short period of time (see *Rider Fitness: Body & Brain* by Eckart Meyners).

All exercises can be performed on the longe line or on a horse being led.

1) Head and Neck Area
Moving the Head in All Directions
Move your head several times in many different ways. If possible, do not repeat any direction. You should utilize all movement options (to the front, to the side, to the back, tucking it in, and stretching it upward). There is no limit to your imagination!

Head and Eyes in Opposite Directions
Move your head to the right and to the left. While doing this, your eyes look in the opposite direction. Repeat 10 times each way.

Loosen up the head, neck, and nape of the neck by moving the head in all directions.

Basic Elements: Balance and Aids

1 *Turn your head one way, and look the other.*

2 *Release tension by massaging the space between your skull and your first cervical vertebra.*

Hold your arm in front of you and focus your gaze on your hand as you rotate your torso right and left.

Massage and Stretch the Atlanto-Occipital Joint

You can release tension around the occipital joint by performing this massage exercise. Use your ring, middle, and index fingers of both hands to massage the area between the skull and the first cervical vertebra.

Variation: After massaging, you can perform a stretch: Rest the tip of your left middle finger on the occipital joint; place the tip of the right middle finger on the middle finger of the left hand. Stretch your elbows out to the side and put pressure on the joint.

2) Breastbone and Rib Cage
Axial Rotation While Focusing on Your Hand

Hold your right arm in front of you at shoulder level then bend your elbow at an almost 90-degree angle and lower your wrist with your hand loosely hanging down. The hand should be approximately 20 inches (50cm) from your eyes.

During the entire exercise, direct your gaze toward your wrist. Now turn your upper body—looking at your hand—as far to the right and left as possible without straining. Repeat the exercise 10 times then switch arms to perform the same exercise.

Hugging Yourself

Sitting on the horse, place your right hand on your left shoulder so that the elbow is placed on your chest. Slide your left hand between your chest and right arm up to the right shoulder. Your right elbow now rests on your left arm, and your left elbow on the chest. With both hands resting on your shoulders, move your elbows up into a horizontal position and higher, keeping focused on your elbows. The movement should feel pleasant: Do not strain to overcome resistance. Repeat the entire process up to 10 times, then switch arms and repeat an additional 10 times.

Cross your arms as you did in the first step, lift your elbows into the horizontal position and move them as far to the right and to the left as possible without straining. Focus on your elbows during this movement as well. Then change the arm position.

Now cross the arms again. Bring your elbows into the horizontal position and from there take them in a soft arc once to the upper right, then to the upper left. For this exercise as well, let your eyes follow the movement of your elbows. Then change the arm position.

Using your hands to pull your shoulders in various directions creates flexibility in your entire upper body.

3) Muscle and Tendon Reflexes (Golgi tendon organ)
Trapezius and Pectoral Muscles

Tension in the shoulder can be released by "plucking" the trapezius muscle (it lifts the shoulder) with your thumb and index or middle finger. You can stimulate your pectoral muscles (chest muscles) in the same way.

Note: In the beginning, these "plucking" exercises may feel uncomfortable, but this will improve when you practice it daily.

Pinching or "plucking" your shoulders daily can quickly dissolve tension in the shoulder.

Hip Flexors (psoas major and iliacus muscles)

You can reduce the strong reflexes that control the hip flexors (the skeletal muscles that move the thigh bone) by "relaxing" or stretching them. As a result, the pelvis is able to better go with the horse's movement since it will no longer be tipping forward. You can feel the iliacus when you lift your foot so the hip flexor is contracted. Use your finger tips to perform massage-type rubbing movements from left to right and back across the muscle/tendon strand (see photos). If it feels uncomfortable, go slowly and carefully increase the pressure. When carried out every day, this exercise helps to make the hip flexor more flexible.

The inner hip flexors (iliacus muscles, adductors) can be relaxed by performing the plucking massage exercise: Sit on the horse with legs slightly spread away from the seat and palpate the entire muscle/tendon strand from the knees to the pubic bone in the pinching, "plucking" fashion as described above. (In the beginning, this can lead to bruising because the soft tissue may be "stuck" together due to myofascial adhesions.)

Stimulating the hip flexor creates a flexible pelvis.

4) The Sacroiliac Joint and Pelvic Mobility
Mobilization Exercises
Sitting Dynamically on One Buttock

Sitting on a horse is never rigid (static)—it is always *dynamic*. You can break through the stereotypical seating pattern by sliding one buttock down the side and out of the saddle, then gently lifting and lowering this free side of the body 8 to 12 times. (Repeat on the other side.) You will feel this change as a pleasant reorganization of your entire body structure.

The Face of a Clock

Sitting on the horse, imagine you are sitting on the face of a clock: when you lower the pelvis to the right, you are sitting on three o'clock, and when you lower it to the left, you are sitting on nine o'clock. You can perform these two movements either on one side only or you can combine them in one fluid motion. Vary the pace of your movements: The motion should be performed fluidly and without strain (see Meyners, 2009).

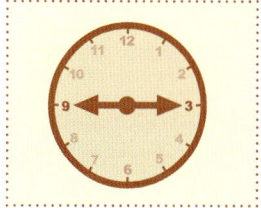

Mobilize the pelvis by lifting and lowering it on the left and right side.

5) Flexibility in the Large Joints
Moving the Shoulders in all Directions
Lift the shoulder, lower it; then combine both movements. Move the shoulder forward, then back, and combine the movement. Do it on both sides then perform circular shoulder movements going both ways.

Circular Movements with "Long" Legs from the Hip Joint
Take your feet out of the stirrups and move them in a circular motion clockwise and counter-clockwise. While doing so, keep changing the size of the circles in order to integrate all the muscles that attach to the

All shoulder movements should be repeated between 8 and 12 times.

Shoulder movements in all directions increase the mobility of the shoulder girdle.

hip joint into the movement. You can add to the exercise by either stretching or bending your toes.

The hip joint can be mobilized by various leg movements, as can the pelvis (photos below.)

Cycling (Forward and Backward)
Take your feet out of the stirrups and perform cycling movements forward and backward, moving one or both legs at a time.

6) Cross-Coordination Movement
Cross-coordination movements prepare the rider for an optimal seat. Turning the shoulders against the pelvis, and twisting and touching the toes with your hand on alternate sides, support your ability to adapt to various situations while on the horse. You will learn how to keep your shoulders parallel to the horse's shoulders and your pelvis parallel to his, also.

Turning the Shoulders Against the Hips
Perform *active* movements with your shoulders and turn them in the opposite direction to your hips.

This exercise can also be performed with *passive* shoulder movements by placing your hands on both shoulder joints and pulling the shoulders in the opposite direction of the pelvis. Cross your arms in front of your chest and place your hands on your shoulder joints. With the help of your hands, turn your shoulders to the left while moving your left hip to the right, and vice versa.

1 With shorter stirrups, twist the body as shown. This exercise helps you to find a good position in the saddle.

2 Touching your left foot with your right hand, and vice versa, also helps your saddle position.

Twisting in the "Monkey" Position

Shorten the stirrups considerably and assume the "monkey" pose (forward seat, see p. 34). Make twisting motions—your pelvis rotates opposite your shoulders while your arms and hands follow the motion of your shoulders, crossing your body's midline.

Left Hand Touches Right Foot and Vice Versa

This exercise is performed with opposing torque. Alternately touch one foot with the opposite arm. Let your eyes follow the movement. Do this several times.

The Rider's Aids

Once the rider is able to stay in balance and relaxed while letting herself be moved by the horse, she must learn to apply the essential body-language signals that enable her to communicate with the horse—the aids.

At the beginning of a rider's education, the goal is to understand which aids are available and how they are basically executed and applied. Only at a more advanced stage of the rider's basic education can she apply a complex interplay of aids in such a way that they will have a targeted—and intended—effect on the way the horse moves.

During the course of the rider's education she will gain insight into the fact that there is a structure between the driving and the restraining aids, which are always in correlation to one another. However, to confront the beginner with this complexity is too much to ask, so we will therefore—just like in an actual riding lesson—exclusively talk about which aids there are and how the rider should apply them. Later, we will use practical examples to take a closer look at the interplay of the aids, the relationship of the driving and restraining aids and of unilateral and bilateral weight, leg, and rein aids and their effects on the horse.

Basically, we differentiate between three essential types of aids: weight aids, leg aids, and rein aids. All three are in constant

There are three essential body-language signals available to the rider: weight, leg, and rein aids. The rider's weight should be the predominant aid. All three types of aids are always given in correlation to one another: They should not be given in isolation but be coordinated.

interaction. Nevertheless, the rider must be able to induce each of them independently, which can only be successfully done when the rider is in balance.

Weight Aids

Of the three basic aids, the rider's weight aid is the most natural. It can occur *unilaterally* or *bilaterally*, and both can "load" or "unload" the horse's back. The rider uses the weight aid to prompt the horse to change his tempo, shape (frame), and direction of travel. The weight aid is a mechanical way of transferring the movement of the rider's weight, that is, influence by means of the pelvis, onto the horse.

Example: When the rider shifts her body to the right, the horse will follow her change in balance and turn to the right.

Conclusion: It is this weight function that the rider should work with the most. Tipping her pelvis forward, which intentionally "unloads" the horse's body, signals him to move forward. Tilting the pelvis backward—thus "loading" the horse's back—always reduces the activity in the horse's back and, therefore, has the effect of slowing him down.

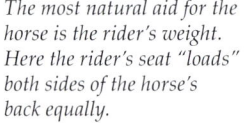

The most natural aid for the horse is the rider's weight. Here the rider's seat "loads" both sides of the horse's back equally.

The Rider's Aids

In this context, it is often said that the rider doesn't tilt the pelvis forward but rather leans forward with her upper body. This, however, is anatomically and physiologically incorrect (in the functional sense). This movement originates in the pelvis and only as a result of it can the upper body slightly tip forward and backward (see below).

Physical Preconditions for Being Able to Give Correct Weight Aids
Bilateral Weight Aid

The *bilateral* weight aid can only be given when the rider is sitting upright with her spine in a double-S curve. Here, the rider's pelvis must be tilted a bit to the front (resulting in a slightly hollow back) so that the pelvis can—in accordance with the trot motion of the horse—lower to the same extent on the right and left, and at the same time move forward and back. Note these are *reactive*, not *active* movements.

This pelvis motion to the front and back is also important in the canter so you don't inhibit the horse's back movement, when he raises or lowers it. It is only under these conditions that your two seat bones can continuously have an optimal *bilateral* effect. When the rider's pelvis is equally flexible to the front and back, she can develop

> **First the Pelvis, Then the Upper Body**
>
> In order to be able to give weight aids that load the horse differently, the rider must be flexible in the pelvis because it is the pelvis that tips forward or back. The upper body can easily follow the movement of the pelvis.

Especially when on a young horse, a rider should repeatedly "unload" the horse's back during a lesson as this rider is doing here in combination with praising him. This is pure motivation!

Basic Elements: Balance and Aids

A Balimo Chair Represents the Horse's Back

The Balimo (Balance in Motion) chair is a tool to help a person develop better and more conscious body awareness (see www.balimochairs.com). This improved awareness has an impact on riding. The Balimo, however, is not intended to be a simulation of the horse's back and, therefore, should not be used as a "riding simulator" during riding instruction.

a feel for the center position of the pelvis, that is, a *neutral* position, slightly tilted forward.

The Balimo Chair as a Learning Aid

Since many riders are "blocked" in the pelvis, it is possible to reactivate three-dimensional movement by sitting on a Balimo chair. Only when a rider has regained this ability can she sense the horse's back movement and influence him with her targeted weight aids.

On the Balimo, it is impossible not to move, meaning that you sit—just as on the horse—in constant motion. This is necessary in order to provide the entire body with natural vacillation; these undulations are transferred from the pelvis—the "motor" of the human body—to the head and to the feet. Sensitive vacillations challenge and stimulate your perception through increased mobility of the pelvis: The greater the variety of pelvic movement, the better the entire body is brought into an erect position.

Therefore, the Balimo chair is a tool that helps people to develop an overall better perception of their own body and body awareness, and to systematically practice the seat aids (both unilateral and bilateral).

The Balimo chair enhances the mobility of the pelvis in all directions. When tilting the pelvis from right to left (from three to nine o'clock), this also has an effect on the upper body and the legs.

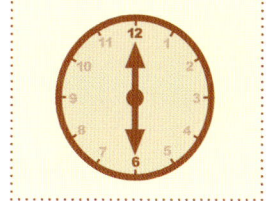

This rider is very flexible in the forward-back exercises as well as sideways. Later, in the saddle, he will easily be able to follow the movements of the horse's back.

These exercises should be performed in a slow and soft manner. By varying the speed and effort, your brain will learn to react flexibly: Speed should be predominantly slow to enable the brain to follow the movements, which enhances their quality.

Sit on the Balimo, place your hands on your thighs or let them hang down your sides. Have your feet at shoulder-width, with your body forming four almost right angles: feet to lower leg; lower leg to thigh; thigh to upper body; upper body to jaw. Your knees may be positioned a bit lower than the hip joints, but never higher.

This rider is imagining a clock's face underneath his seat (see photo). When he lowers his pelvis to the right, he sits at three o'clock. When he lowers it to the left, he is sitting on nine o'clock. These two movements can be performed to one side only or combined in one fluid movement.

Vary the pace of the movement. It should be possible to touch a ring that is installed under the chair's seat—without straining, however—which makes a clicking sound when you do. Tilt your pelvis to the front to twelve o'clock then back, to six o'clock. Both movements should be combined. (Also see Meyners, 2005).

The unilateral weight aid is not only necessary for transitioning into the canter, but also for maintaining the canter. In the process, the inside hip rolls diagonally forward. As a result, knee and heel are lowered.

> **When the Pelvis "Rolls"**
>
> For many riders, giving a unilateral weight aid is extremely difficult (see p. 50 for unilateral versus bilateral aids). It is a "rolling" movement that comes from the pelvis—not a "tilting" to the right or left. When the rider is able to give a unilateral weight aid with the pelvis in a rolling movement, for instance, when transitioning into the canter, the result is an automatic "deep" knee and an overall relaxed leg.

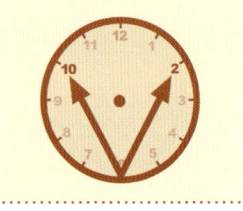

Unilateral Weight Aid

Most riders are not aware how a unilateral weight aid should be applied. Many horses, for instance, transition into the canter solely as a reaction to the impulse given by the rider's outside leg—and frequently, the rider is not applying a weight aid. Other riders go to apply the weight aid, but collapse in the hip in the process. Moving the inside hip forward is also not the solution since the outside shoulder automatically goes back, and as a result, the rider is unable to follow the horse's movement.

None of the riding theories explain how the physiological sequence of the unilateral weight aid should be carried out. But it is relatively easy to learn the process on the Balimo: Imagining the face of a clock underneath you, "roll" into the direction of the 6 and then directly (without making any "evasive" movements to the side) to the front in the direction of the left knee, which on the clock is 10. The same sequence can be performed in the direction of the right knee, in which case, you are on the 2.

We must point out how many riders perform "evasive" movements during this direct "rolling" movement, meaning that they roll from 6, over 7, 8, and 9 to 10, or from 6 over 5, 4, and 3 to 2.

When the unilateral weight aid is correctly performed on the Balimo chair, the respective knee automatically goes forward. On the horse, the knee lowers itself.

Leg Aids

Beginners initially learn about the leg aids as *driving* aids. Often, however, the leg aid is misunderstood to be a constant pressure: Intending to drive the horse forward, the rider continuously uses her hamstrings (*biceps femoris*), which often leads to her "clamping" with her lower leg. This just "pesters" the horse and actually has a *slowing* effect (by desensitizing him) and can lead to the horse becoming lazy.

At the other end of the spectrum is so-called "impulse" riding where the rider only gives a leg aid when the horse slows down. In the classical riding theory, however, the driving leg aids are impulses that should be given as rarely as possible, but as often as necessary.

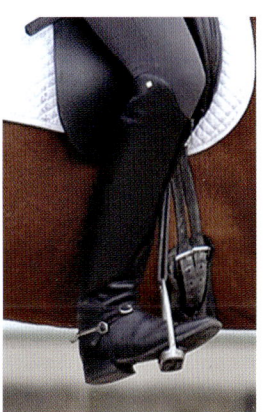

The rider must let the entire leg fall loosely from the hip and rest the foot in the stirrup for support in order to enable the legs to "breathe" with the horse.

In principle, the goal of a driving aid is to motivate the horse to become *active* in his hindquarters and to step toward the rider's hand. The result of a driving aid can be a change in tempo *or* increased collection.

Correct driving is made up of a very complex combination of movements. It is not simply about moving your calf to the horse's side by using the hamstrings and initiating an impulse, but it is just as important to let the entire leg fall loosely from the hip *after* this driving impulse. Your foot—supported by the stirrup under the widest part of the ball of the foot—should "give" elastically and reactively as a result of a flexible hip joint. Having your stirrups too long, or actively looking for support in the stirrups, inhibits suppleness and a "driving" ability. The entire leg must be draped alongside the horse in a relaxed fashion in order to enable the leg to "breathe" with the horse.

You can find exercises to feel and learn correct driving aids from page 52 onward.

The horse reacts to the driving message with forward movement in the walk, trot, or canter. Now is when you utilize a natural reflex of the horse, which occurs as follows: The elastic touch of your calf on the horse's abdomen initiates a muscle contraction that prompts the horse to more actively move the respective hind leg. (Bürger/ Zietzschmann, page 33).

From Unconditional to Conditional Reflex

During the basic schooling of the young horse, this natural reflex must be engrained in him by means of targeted exercises. A type of conditioning based on natural reflex, this is an *unconditional* reflex—as opposed to a *conditional* (i.e. learned) reflex. With a *unilateral* driving aid, the horse learns to step forward with the hind leg when he is touched in the belly by the rider's leg. A *bilateral* driving aid is when both the rider's legs, left and right, touch the horse's body, and the horse steps forward equally with both legs.

When the rider is able to bring the horse's legs into different positions, he can influence the action of the horse's hindquarters. For instance, he can prompt a hind leg to step under the horse's center of gravity.

Here is an example: Every rider who has taken a few lessons,

Natural Reflex

Initially, the horse's reaction to the rider's driving aid is a natural reflex. Through continuous exercise, this reflex becomes engrained in the horse and can later be used by the rider in a more accomplished fashion.

Each of the rider's leg movements triggers a reflex in the horse that the rider can utilize. Clearly visible in this image sequence: The rider is getting the horse to line up properly and load all four legs equally by using his driving aids.

knows this situation: Having come to a full halt, the horse is not lined up properly on all four legs but has "parked out" a hind leg. In order to correct this, an impulse (aid) given by the rider's leg against the horse's body on the same side can ensure that the hind leg that's left behind is prompted to step forward. This is the exact situation where the above—described reflex of the horse can be utilized.

Basically, the rider must learn that her leg movements trigger a reaction in the horse so she must learn to maintain her balance with foresight. Her pelvis must follow the horse's movement reactively (not actively) and with suppleness. In order to develop a feel for this, it can be helpful at the beginning of each riding session to ride a few transitions from walk to halt then move off again at a walk.

The Leg's Function

The leg function, however, is not only for driving the horse forward. It can also be used as a *guarding* aid and a *forward-and-sideways* driving aid. Depending on how the rider uses her leg, she is able to trigger three different responses:
- Driving forward
- Driving forward and sideways
- Guarding (limiting sideways movement)

Depending on its necessary function, a rider must bring it into different positions. This positioning is not a "formal" requirement; instead its position is a functional necessity resulting from the anatomical and physiological realities of both rider and horse. The lesson

The rider's correct leg position is a function of what the leg needs to do at this moment in time; it is not being used like this because of some "formal" riding position requirement. In the photo on the left, the inside left leg has a guarding (sideways-limiting) function, which is why it is behind the girth. In the photo on the right, however, it is positioned at the girth in its driving function.

being taught and general situation determines how actively the leg should be applied.

A basic operating principle is that the *driving* leg is applied at the girth to trigger forward movement of the hind leg. The *guarding* leg should be positioned one-hand's width behind the girth. When in this place, it prompts the hind leg to *lift up* instead of just stepping forward. Depending on what the rider intends to trigger in the horse, she must, therefore, position her calf on the horse's side in alignment with the function: farther forward or farther back. The formal teaching description that the driving aid is always given at the girth and the guarding or forward-sideways aid are always given one-hand's width behind the girth does not always fulfill the requirements of the riding situation at the time.

Driving Correctly

In order for the calf to trigger a reflex in the horse to activate the hindquarters, the rider must use her thigh musculature with elasticity (but also sensitivity). Utilizing this musculature causes the rider to briefly increase the bend in her knee, thus automatically touching the horse with the calf. This process, however, must occur with rhythm, meaning that while driving, the rider's rear thigh musculature is alternately contracted and relaxed, which induces an activation of the horse's hind legs.

Driving can be misunderstood, as is observed in many riders who "drive" every step in the walk, trot, and canter (p. 51); the horse's abdominal muscles are continuously being stimulated, which leads to dullness and lack of suppleness. The rider is not working with the back of the thigh's musculature but instead is using the *gastrocnemius* muscles located in the back of the knee, underneath the hollow part. Using this muscle automatically leads to a high heel. Caused by an incorrect understanding of driving, this muscle "jumps into action" before the correct driving muscles can be applied. This type of driving also results in a pulled-up knee.

Many riders also drive incorrectly as a result of the instruction "Toes in". When the rider is expected to drive from this leg and foot position (being told to "Drive with your calf"), she can only touch the horse by contracting the adductors, a process that leads to spasm, locks the pelvis, prevents the rider from sitting supply, and blocks the horse's back (also see Meyners, 2005).

A pulled-up heel (see small photo) is an indication that the rider is driving incorrectly with the gastrocnemius muscles. The correct way is to use the rear thigh muscles (see arrow, large photo).

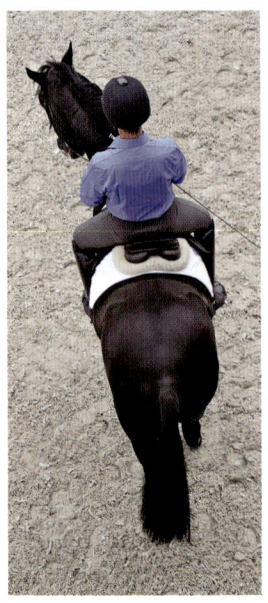

In order to frame the horse correctly during a turn with the driving aids, the inside leg should be positioned farther forward than the outside leg. Therefore, the inside calf is driving on the girth while the outside calf is guarding behind the girth.

Furthermore, many riders ride with pulled-up heels. The pulled-up heel is a weakness that is created by the fact that nobody has ever explained to the rider how the process of driving actually works. Driving correctly, proper use of the rear thigh musculature automatically results in a low heel. When the rear thigh is used correctly, rhythmically, the heel will be "springy" as a result (provided that the hip joint is free).

Exercises for the Driving Motion Pattern

The rider lies down in face-down position. Her hips should ideally be slightly elevated by means of a pad so that she cannot hollow her back when using the knee flexors. The legs are stretched out. Now she bends one knee and brings the heel to the buttocks. Initially, this sequence should be performed slowly in order to create awareness around this movement. Later, she can perform this motion pattern at greater speed and velocity, yet with sensitivity, resembling the driving movement on the horse.

When the rider pulls up the heel and points her toe out, she is incorrectly using the *gastrocnemius* muscles, located in the area of the hollow at the back of the knee. When she drives correctly though, her calf muscles will be naturally toned by means of the rear thigh musculature, which makes the rider unconsciously pull up the tip of her foot.

In this context, it becomes clear that an instructor must know which movement is *actively* produced and which one occurs *reactively* (automatically). When the rider actively pushes the heel down or consciously pulls up the tip of the foot while driving forward (therefore involving additional musculature) the natural transfer of the rider's movement onto the horse (ability to give correct leg aids) is no longer possible. Tension develops in the rider, her movements are out of rhythm, and the horse is hardly able to interpret them as unambiguous aids.

Rein Aids

Rein aids are the most multi-faceted and also the ones most difficult to learn. Basically, the rider's hand creates the connection to the horse's sensitive mouth. This connection, it should be understood, is as a result of the effect created in the horse by the interplay of all the rider's

Exercises for the Driving Motion Pattern

- The rider lies face down as shown, his legs extended. There should be a small pad under the hip. The legs are slightly apart and one by one, each heel is moved toward the buttocks, then lowered again.

- A helper can gently push her hand against the lower part of the "driving" leg to create resistance. This resistance can be increased depending on the rider's strength.

- Another option: Instead of using a hand to provide resistance, the helper can also use an exercise band or a sturdy bicycle tube: The rider lies face down as above, the exercise band is wrapped around the ankle of the extended leg with the other end tied to an object. The rider can now continuously pull the ankle toward the buttocks. Also, the rider can increase the resistance or her effort by moving farther away from the object.

The Driving Motion Pattern

In order to drive correctly, the rider must contract and relax her rear thigh musculature. It is easy to practice this with the exercise described in the sidebar.

aids. Weight and leg aids trigger movements in the horse that travel through the entire body and practically "arrive" at the horse's mouth. So again, it is about interweaving various possibilities in the application of aids.

While we will initially describe rein aids here as an isolated topic, they must, however, *never* be given as an *isolated aid*. Rein aids are always the result of a targeted interplay of weight and leg aids orchestrated by the rider, and all three of them must be coordinated together.

In order to be able to give effective rein aids, it is essential that the rider has found her balance on the horse and does not have to "find support on" or "hold onto" the reins.

In principle, rein aids can help to point the horse in a direction of travel, influence the horse's self-carriage, and have a slowing effect. We differentiate between *asking, yielding, non-yielding* (retaining), and *sidewise-acting* (opening) rein aids. In addition, they can be applied

The goal of holding the reins in the proper manner is to create a continuous, elastic connection between the rider's hand and the horse's mouth. When giving and retaking the reins (see photo on the left) this connection is briefly abandoned, but when letting the horse "chew" the reins out of her hands, the rider maintains a continuous, soft connection.

unilaterally or *bilaterally*. The goal of holding the reins and of all rein aids is to create a continuous, elastic connection between the rider's hand and the horse's mouth.

If you take a closer look at the description in *The Principles of Riding* that pertains to the correct manner of holding the reins, it will seem very formal. However, there is a functional background for each and every requirement. These formal requirements are meant to enable maximum flexibility of the rider.

Upper Arm

The upper arm should hang loosely from the upper body; its vertical line should not get behind or in front of the upper body.

The Reason: When the upper arms are in the hanging position, all muscles in the area of the shoulder joint are relaxed. It is only from this relaxed musculature that the rider can develop a sensitive feel in order to give the respective impulses (i.e. aids) with the reins. Any tension equals effort, which hinders feel.

Lower Arm

Together with the back of the hand and the reins, the forearm should form one line to the horse's mouth.

The Reason: This requirement basically results from the structure of the forearm. It is only possible to apply fine and well-"dosed" aids from the wrist when all the muscles of the forearm are as long and relaxed as possible. When the knuckles point in or out, the wrist is prevented from applying a soft aid because the forearm is tensed.

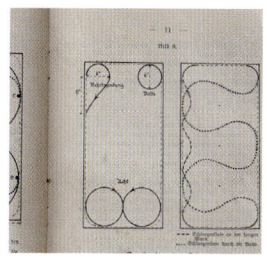

In order to be able to give finely tuned rein aids, the forearm must point toward the horse's mouth. Only then is the forearm musculature relaxed. The rider in the left photo shows the correct way; the rider on the right is contracting both biceps muscles and consequently her forearms are held too high.

Fist

The fingers should be closed, not clenched or open.

The Reason: The hand must be closed to make a soft fist without using any effort that could tense up the fingers that rest in a relaxed position one above the other, with the thumb on top. From this hand position it is possible to softly—actively or reactively—contract and relax the fingers. This is not possible if the rider abandons this fist position to open the fingers slightly; this hand posture has a rigid and hard effect, the fingers become braced and tense, and cannot give soft aids. Many riders think that this hand position will help them to give more careful and sensitive aids to the horse's mouth, but it's a misconception.

Thumbs

The thumb should rest on top of the fist, in the shape of a roof.
The Reason: In this position you can press the thumb (in the "roof" shape) firmly down in order to prevent the rein from slipping

through, without needing to strongly contract the forearm flexor, which would cause a "blocking" effect on the wrist. If the thumb, however, is pressed down in a *flat* shape, the forearm-flexor musculature contracts to such an extent that the rider will no longer be able to use her wrist in a softly yielding or retaining manner.

Auxiliary Means Are Not Aids

Of course there are additional signals to make the horse understand what the rider wants. But incorrectly, these other means of communication—such as the voice—are also called "aids." It is possible to condition a horse so he will slow down when he hears a drawn-out sound like "Whoooaaa," or even learn to stop when he hears it and often the voice is used while educating the horse during groundwork for it's a good method when schooling young horses. The voice can continue to be used until the horse has learned the three basic aids. However, voice support is not an aid in classical riding theory since it cannot be used to stimulate coordinated movement in the horse.

Additional well-known auxiliary means are spurs and the whip, which we mention here only for the sake of being complete. While the whip can help to teach the horse the driving-leg aids, the spur can be an aid for refining the leg aids (differentiation and immediacy) for advanced riders and horses. This is reflected in the rules and standards of the sport at the higher levels. For example, in international dressage, the voice aid is prohibited, as is the riding whip. Riding with spurs, however, is mandatory.

> **The Difference Between Aids and Auxiliary Means**
>
> Weight, leg, and rein aids are body-language signals that prompt the horse to perform specific motion patterns. Spurs, voice, and whip are auxiliary means that have no more than a supporting effect.

Outlook: The Interplay of Aids

In riding literature, there is often mention of the "symphony" of aids. This means that the rider must be able to apply each one of the previously described aids in varying degrees of intensity, and, most of all, coordinate them with one another. During the rider's basic education, the aspect of "the symphony of aids" is often not given enough consideration. We can't help but observe in many riders that the weight aids are reduced to tilting the upper body forward, backward, and to the sides, instead of tilting the pelvis. The leg aid is reduced to a minimally coordinated "pounding" of the leg on the horse's belly, and the rein aids to pulling the horse's head to the left or right.

At the beginning of her education, it is vital for the rider to understand that the three essential aids must always, at all times, in every gait, and during every lesson, be applied in conjunction with each other and in a coordinated fashion.

Independent Aids

In order for the rider to be able to give her aids independently, yet in coordination with each other, she must learn—from the kinetics perspective—to perform or coordinate several movement patterns simultaneously. At the beginning, this is easier to do when the horse

The more complicated the lesson, the more important it is that the rider is able to apply his aids in a coordinated fashion. Dressage movements like travers, as seen in the photos, and renvers require the rider to competently be able to use coordinated aids.

Doing trot work, the conversation between this rider and a young horse is not yet at its best. The flow of movement from his back end to his front needs to gain a greater influence on his posture, and his poll should become the highest point of his body.

When doing canter work, it is easier for the horse to implement the rider's aids. Here you can see the horse's hindquarters step more actively underneath his body, his shoulder has more range of motion, and his neck and poll are being "carried" better.

is being led or on the longe line since the rider can exclusively focus on learning the necessary coordination. Without this extra security provided, it's hard to experience the coordination of aids: It's important to prepare a rider—by practicing with reins and stirrups—for the "real world" of riding on her own.

Only when the rider is in balance and rhythm can she perform the various aids independently and in a coordinated fashion. When she is still looking for balance, she cannot perform several movement patterns at the same time, or one after another. Every rider who has difficulty giving aids should first work to stabilize her balance (see the exercises on pp. 35–42). When this is done, she will realize that it is easier to give the aids.

At a Glance

- There is a difference between a rider's ability and her skill. Ability is not strictly related to one type of sport; it is the basic foundation for movement. In equestrian sport, skill is learned through teaching and consists of techniques such as backing up or lateral work.

- In riding sports, balance and rhythm (ability) have a pivotal significance.

- Balance is the ability that forms the basis for learning all movement.

- Various balance exercises can help the rider to solidify this ability.

- Movement Rhythm is defined as the rider's ability to let the horse move her in a relaxed fashion, in order to later move the horse by means of her influence.

- The rider's influence has an effect on three essentials in the horse: gait, direction of movement, and self-carriage.

- In order to influence the horse, the rider uses the three essential aids: weight, leg, and rein. The weight aids are the predominant aids, the leg aids support, while the rein should be the most minimal of the aids.

- The horse can only understand and implement precise aids. For this reason, the rider must resolve any "blockages" in her body that could lead to an imprecise application of aids; she can do this by practicing respective exercises, such as the ones in the 6-Point Program (p. 35).

Basics of Rider Preparation

The Warm-Up

It is still not a matter of course that riders perform a warm-up of themselves before riding. The importance of this preparation for conditioning and coordination is much undervalued. No matter what type of sport you engage in, however, it is only possible to produce a good performance when meaningful and systematic warm-up exercises are performed.

No rider would start a dressage test or ride into a show-jumping course without having warmed up her horse, but almost every rider gets on a horse without having warmed up herself.

In the following pages, we will explain the reasons for warming up. Shifts in the body's condition are significant and apply to all riders. To some extent, the process is the same in the horse. We will take a detailed look at the warm-up exercises in this chapter.

Effects on the Heart Rate

Warming up the body increases activity in its entire circulation, which enables a better performance. Transitioning from a stationary phase to a "stress" phase should not be abrupt but fluid, since physical-performance capability does not kick in for approximately 30 seconds. For a trained athlete, this first phase, in which the cardiovascular system is stimulated and the metabolic hormone adrenaline is released, is a bit shorter than it is for the untrained person. After this, in the second phase, the metabolic processes are optimally refined. In order to ensure that both phases occur with efficiency, both rider and horse must be carefully prepared.

Rise in Body Temperature

During a warm-up, the body, muscle, and skin temperature rises. This rise in body temperature goes along with metabolic changes. During longer riding sessions, perspiration creates an increased loss of fluids: It evaporates and produces a chill, which lowers skin and body temperature. Normal metabolic processes occurs at a body temperature of around 98.6° F (37° C). In the arms and legs, the temperature can be up to 9° F (5° C) lower. This difference has a negative impact on the performance of the rider's seat and consequently, her

In equestrian sports, rider warm-up is still not done as a matter of course. But when the rider is not warmed up, she makes it unnecessarily hard for her and the horse to find harmony.

aids. The best conditions for rider performance exist with a body temperature of 101–102° F (38.5 to 39° C.)

Respiratory System

During the warm up, the number of breaths increase as does their depth, since the oxygen demand of the working musculature increases and the accumulated metabolic waste products must be removed.

Usually, there is a delay in the acceleration of respiration after any "stress" begins. In the case of endurance stress, the "steady state," meaning the state in which energy input and energy output are balanced, is not reached until after a certain period of time.

The less stamina a rider has, the earlier she enters the anaerobic phase, in which her body enters a state of oxygen deficiency. The "steady state" is no longer. This automatically leads to a loss of coordination and the rider is no longer able to correctly influence the horse. Consequently, the horse may make mistakes.

Warming up counteracts the above described "start delay," so that respiration is elevated to a sufficient base level before the actual stress starts, meaning the rider is already prepared (the same applies to the horse).

Minimizing Internal Muscle Friction

Elevated muscle temperature minimizes internal muscle friction. This is important in order to prevent tension, spasm, and injury. Furthermore, warming up the body first increases the elasticity of muscles and the mobility of muscles and joints. Especially in colder climes, an increased body temperature helps to minimize the risk of injury.

Effect on Coordination and Riding Technique

The rise in body temperature that occurs during a warm-up minimizes internal muscles' friction and, at the same time, increases their elasticity and extension. As a direct result, the nervous system and the muscles are better able to interact. Improved coordination—the interaction of all muscles—lowers energy consumption, and the entire body is slower to fatigue.

The working muscles' increased ability to relax has an especially

During cross-coordination exercises, the shoulders and pelvis are "twisted" in opposite directions. This makes it easier for the rider to sit on the horse so that her pelvis remains parallel to the horse's pelvis, and her shoulders are parallel to the horse's shoulders.

"Rolling" movements mobilize the rider's spine.

positive effect during quick, fine coordination movement patterns like flying lead changes, tempi changes, or lateral movements, for example.

The performance speed of the nerve pathways is increased and makes the receptors on muscles, tendons, and joints especially sensitive. As a result, the latency period—the time that passes between nerve impulses and muscle reaction—is shortened and movement awareness is refined, which enables more precise aids. This means the rider is quicker to perceive physical sensations.

Preparation of the Capsule, Ligament, Tendon, and Cartilage Tissue

Higher body temperatures also pay an essential role in the body's fascia. Just as it does for the cardiovascular system, the adjustment happens slowly—even more so with fascia. Optimal elasticity and plasticity of the fibers of joint capsules, ligaments, tendons, and cartilage tissue are not achieved until body temperature reaches 102–104° F (39 to 40° C). Due to slower metabolic speed, preparation of cartilage takes longer than warming up the musculature since these two types of tissue have completely different flexibility.

The joint cartilage is nourished exclusively by synovial fluid and is not directly connected to the blood system. Synovial fluid is created in the synovium and from there is funneled into the interior of the

> **Warm-up**
> The warm-up is of significant importance for body and mind during which negative tension can be minimized or even completely dissolved.

joint. By warming up, you can improve nourishment inside the joint cartilage, and after a while, the cartilage layer in the joints thickens.

After moving a joint for five minutes, the cartilage-nourishing synovial fluid increases—a process that is concluded after about 20 minutes. This is especially important for athletic performance since it enables the rider to better cushion the horse's forces and, therefore, prevent the risk of injury in the short and the long term.

The production of a sufficient amount of synovial fluid is just as vitally important for the horse. The horse should move at the walk for at least 15 minutes before any actual suppling work starts.

Psychological Effects

Besides the above-mentioned physical-optimizing processes, the warm-up also has a positive psychological effect on the rider and leads to emotional stability. The warm-up counteracts any state of excitement or inhibition, meaning that it serves as a kind of release valve. This valve function is especially important during competition in order to not disturb your—and, therefore, the horse's too—movement patterns due to any trembling or spasms.

Overall, a solid preparation leads to a state of psychological activation: The rider is mentally, physically, and emotionally alert and the horse also becomes attuned to his task when he is systematically prepared beforehand.

This way, the rider creates the best possible conditions for learning, practicing, and training.

> **Learning, Practicing, Training**
>
> - **Learning** is the process of acquiring motion patterns—initially starting with simple movements—that the rider has not yet got in her repertoire.
>
> - **Practicing** is the application of the movements in constantly changing and increasingly complex situations (no monotonous repetition). This requires the rider to be physically fit.
>
> - The main focus of **training** is on increasing fitness so that the practice process can slowly be expanded.
>
> - All three processes of learning, practicing, and training are necessary for acquiring new movements—they are reciprocal in nature—even though the focus differs.

Warm-Up Rules

Age

The scope, length, and intensity of a warm-up depend on the age of rider and horse. Older riders and horses must design their warm-up programs more carefully and with a slower progression since the body is not as flexible anymore and the risk of injury increases.

Time of Day

The length of warm-up preparation is influenced by the circadian rhythms of rider and horse. During sleep, individual body functions are slowed down, or completely shut down. In the early morning hours, therefore, it is necessary to warm up longer until rider and

A young, well-conditioned rider needs less time for the warm-up than an older or unfit rider.

> **Warming Up: For How Long?**
>
> Several factors play a role in regard to the length of the warm-up: age and training level of the rider, time of day, ambient temperature, and rider personality.

horse have reached their maximum performance capability. As the day progresses, preparation time shortens. At around 3 pm, blood circulation and body temperature have reached their maximum level; toward the evening they, once again, decrease.

Ambient Temperature / Climate

Different climates have an effect on the length and intensity of a warm-up. High ambient temperatures shorten it, while rain and cold will extend it, though weather-proof clothing can help to shorten the preparation time. Making horse and rider perspire, however, does not replace proper preparation.

Rider Attitude and Personality

The rider's attitude has an effect on the length and effectiveness of the preparation. When the rider views the planned riding activity as especially significant, released hormones facilitate the switch from the resting metabolism to the active metabolism.

Anxiety has a significant effect on the level of tension in the rider's muscles and on the narrowing or dilatation of blood vessels. Her personality determines whether she reacts with increasing or decreasing stress. Overall, preparation has a regulating effect.

Length and Scope of Preparation

The personal training level of the rider determines the length and scope of her individual preparation time. Riders and horses that prepare daily for their tasks require a shorter time period compared to those who only train once a week, for example.

Types of Preparation

General Preparation

During general preparation, the large muscle groups should be activated. If possible, all of the body's muscle groups are involved in order to elevate overall ability to a higher level. In order to prevent fatigue, you should not use muscle groups several times in succession. The best effect is achieved when tasks are as varied as possible.

The rider can perform various exercises to help her solve individual coordination issues and tension, not only before getting on the horse, but also when in the saddle.

Goal: This general preparation has a positive effect on the cardiovascular system because it raises the body temperature, increases respiration, and facilitates the tissues in joint capsules, tendons, ligaments, and cartilage.

Special Preparation

The warm-up phase is directly connected to the rider's next task: actually riding the horse. In this context, the 6-Point Program becomes relevant (see p. 35). In addition, you can include any special problem areas. For the horse, consider the aspects discussed from page 125 onward.

Goal: To minimize inner-muscle friction, reduce muscle tension and blockages, and prepare for the coordination processes.

The Rider's Mental Preparation

The importance of mental preparation is often underestimated. During training, you mentally perform the movements, that is, you "see" or visualize the movement's sequence in your mind's eye.

This is also called the *Carpenter effect* or *ideomotor effect*, when a subject makes motions unconsciously. William Benjamin Carpenter's research showed that a human being who "sees" a movement that he already knows how to perform can perform it instinctively.

A motion pattern that is performed simultaneously on the right and left sides is called "parallel movements." This particular mounted exercise engages both cerebral hemispheres and has an excellent effect on the large muscles in your arms and shoulders.

The external image is perceived by the eye, which then leads the body to internally perform the movement. So-called ideomotor reactions occur just by imagining the movement, meaning the same biochemical processes occur in the body as during the real riding situation. As said, the prerequisite is that the rider already knows how to perform the basic structure of the movement.

Goal: Plans for movement can be refined so that the quality of the result is improved.

Active Regeneration— The Cool-Down Process

After intense physical exertion, the body must slowly be brought back to its normal state. The mind, soul, and body regenerate during the cool-down process until normal temperature is reached. With the help

> **Motivational Aids for the Warm-Up**
>
> Let's be honest: Who hasn't had a battle with their weaker self? It is that "weaker self" that prevents the rider from warming up—even after having had the experience of how much better, for example, her aids coordination can be. In order to make it easier for you to make it a regular event like brushing your teeth or getting dressed, here are five tips that can really make a difference:
>
> 1. Warming up together is more fun! Meet up with a fellow rider who—just like you—knows that warming up is important.
>
> 2. Look for a suitable place (or a discreet spot, if that helps) in the barn where you can perform your exercises without your horse. Acquire an exercise mat—nobody likes to lie down on a damp or dirty floor.
>
> 3. You can perform many of the warm-up exercises on the horse—use the walk phase at the beginning of your riding session for your 6-Point Program.
>
> 4. Motivate your riding instructor to integrate warm-up exercises into the lesson—all participants will benefit.
>
> 5. We know from experience, that it takes only about 21 days for a human being to internalize a new habit and make it become "second nature." Try to make it through these 21 days and start looking forward to your fellow riders' compliments, for now they will surely notice the visible improvements in your riding!

of the cool-down process, the body exhibits fewer negative signs of stress after training or competition, and is better ready to perform subsequent challenges (see "Warm-Up Routines and Workouts on the Ground" in *Rider Fitness: Body & Brain* by Eckart Meyners).

The Rider's Training Scale

The Horse's Training Scale is considered a necessity, since only against the backdrop of those principles is it possible to school the horse with a rider while keeping his back healthy.

The same, however, applies to the rider: She must also be schooled according to her mind, her psychological and physiological systems.

For a long time, this has not been sufficiently considered during the schooling of the rider. Till this day, one basic problem of riding students is that too little value is attached to the points described in the following chapter, such as trust, suppleness, balance, and rhythm *before* riding.

The Rider's Training Scale is as follows:
1. Trust and fearlessness
2. "Suppleness" (relaxation) of the rider (emotional and physical)
3. Balance and rhythm
4. Movement awareness
5. Proprioception
6. Influence / application of aids / riding technique

Trust
A prerequisite for learning how to ride is *trust*: to trust the horse and instructor. The rider must be fearless. Just as a horse cannot learn if he doesn't trust the rider, the human cannot learn if she doesn't trust her horse and teacher. This is fundamental for learning and improvement in performance and is often ignored. "Don't make such a fuss!" "Suck it up!" "Get over it!" are typical expressions that negate trust.

Suppleness of the Rider
"Suppleness" (relaxation) is the second point of the Rider's Training Scale. The rider must be mentally relaxed: When preoccupied with emotional or other nagging issues—something that an instructor is not always able to notice right away—it is impossible for the rider to ride attentively. "Peace of mind" contributes to physical relaxation.

But suppleness is also reduced by imbalance and temporary tension in individual areas of the rider's body. Three key parts are significant in this context: the neck, the sternum, and the pelvis. These are the most important places that the rider must supple before riding to be better able to follow the horse's movement.

Balance and Rhythm
When the rider's flexibility is increased, there is much less need for the instructor to correct the rider, since she is better able to follow the horse's movement. Being flexible allows her to sit in balance since her muscles no longer tighten up and "pull" against movement. Even before riding, there should be different requirements for the various types of balance (see p. 27). In this way, the rider can avoid having to correct her position using her muscles, since the vestibular (inner ear) and kinesthetic (sense of movement) sys-

This rider and horse are not yet in harmony: The horse is "leaning" on the rider's hand, and the rider has not yet achieved a supple seat.

tems are sensitively prepared for imbalance situations that occur while riding.

Only a rider in balance is able to ride with rhythm. Rhythm and balance are significantly aligned: Balance issues lead to movement that is out of rhythm.

Proprioception

Only when the greatest possible balance and rhythm are created is the rider able to feel her best and, therefore, sensitively influence the

Rider's Training Scale **SUPPLENESS** Rider's ability ⟷ Rider's skill		
Preconditions for the horse	**Preconditions for development of impulsion**	**Preconditions for development of "carrying" power:**
The rider must achieve cognitive, emotional, and movement harmony.	The rider must develop balance, movement, rhythm and proprioception; also be able to give basic aids to support the driving power.	The rider must be able to ride actively, meaning to apply aids and influence in their entire complexity.
The horse should get used to the rider's weight in order to develop Rhythm and Suppleness.	The horse's balance must not be upset, if he is to develop driving power.	Through rider's aids, the horse should be straightened and collected in order to develop carrying power.
Phase 1: **Familiarization**	**Phase 2:** **Development of driving power**	**Phase 3:** **Development of carrying power**

> **Successful Conversation**
> The dialogue between rider and horse will be successful in every stage of education, when both of their "systems" are attuned to one another.

horse. Proprioception (awareness of your body's position) is the fifth point on the Rider's Training Scale and, initially, it means having the ability to follow the horse's movements. The rider must, so to speak, become one with the horse.

Influence/Application of Aids

Only out of the close connection between riding and movement theory is it possible to achieve the ability to influence the horse with precision. The aid must be applied at the right moment and with the right intensity. Aids are technical means to transfer the rider's language to the horse and, therefore, enable a conversation between rider and horse. In a sense, the rider must no longer think about the aids, since the decisive moment of application has often passed by then (also see explanations regarding the Rider's Training Scale in Eckart Meyners' *Rider Fitness: Body & Brain*).

The Rider's Training Scale

On occasion, it can be helpful if the instructor "guides" a movement so that the student can develop the correct feel for how that movement is carried out.

At a Glance

- In order for rider and horse to grow together into one harmonious unit, it must first be clear which abilities and skills the rider must master in order to support the horse in his schooling instead of inhibiting him.

- The Rider's Training Scale must be in context with the Horse's Training Scale.

- Important: A rider with the goal of schooling a horse must be able to meet every requirement of the Rider's Training Scale in order to influence the horse systematically and functionally. Vice versa, it is essential for the beginning rider to experience and feel the Rider's Training Scale with the aid of an experienced and well-schooled horse.

- Only an experienced horse (schoolmaster) is able to teach a rider the complexities of riding movement patterns in regard to balance, rhythm, proprioception, and influence.

Three Fundamental Riding Techniques

Flexion, Bend, and Half-Halts

Using the three fundamental riding techniques of *flexion, bend,* and *half-halts,* the rider develops lessons for gymnasticizing the horse—or, in sports science terminology, she uses them to develop the horse's skills.

In order for the rider to be able to apply these three techniques, she must be able to ride in a coordinated manner using a complex interplay of weight, leg, and rein aids.

Starting right when the horse is first backed, the "conversation" about movement patterns should begin: The rider, because she has already warmed up and thus is more sensitive, should be able to *feel* the range of movement offered by the horse. Based on this feeling and using all her aids, she should be able to precisely influence the horse's gait, posture, and direction of travel.

The term "gymnasticizing" may seem to be of little significance initially; however, it is absolutely fundamental. It means that the horse is made as agile and, from a muscular perspective, as capable as possible (flexible and at the same time stable) by means of the three above mentioned basic riding techniques. The goal is to enable the horse to fulfill any requirements demanded by competition or recreational riding.

Conclusion: When the rider is able to apply flexion, bend, and half-halts, she will be able to ride *all* movements required in classical riding, and be able to transfer from one figure to other figures. For this reason, it will no longer be necessary to repeatedly explain the aids for individual movements such as voltes, serpentines, or riding through corners, for example.

However, a prerequisite for this riding student is an experienced horse familiar with the three techniques described above.

Why Is It Necessary to Flex and Bend?

When you look at the anatomy of the horse you can observe: the shoulders are narrower than the hips. Furthermore, to begin with, every horse is naturally crooked, which means that the hind hoof on one side always steps into the track of the front hoof on the same side, while the hind foot on the other side will step past the front hoof's

---

Gymnastics Keeps the Horse Sound

In order to achieve all the goals of riding (animal welfare, accident prevention, performance ability, and fun), a horse must be properly gymnasticized. For this purpose, the rider has three fundamental riding techniques at her disposal: flexion, bend, and half-halts.

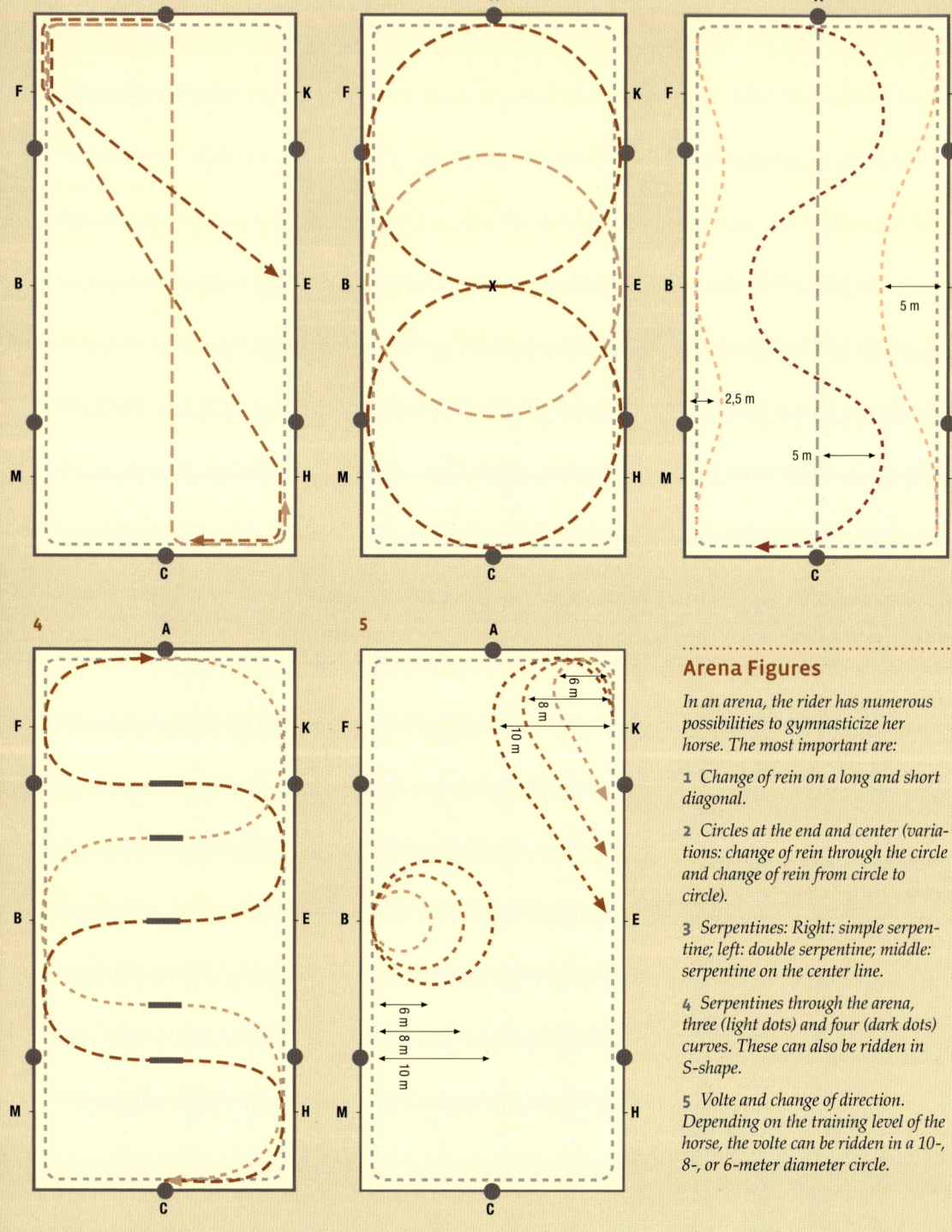

Arena Figures

In an arena, the rider has numerous possibilities to gymnasticize her horse. The most important are:

1 Change of rein on a long and short diagonal.

2 Circles at the end and center (variations: change of rein through the circle and change of rein from circle to circle).

3 Serpentines: Right: simple serpentine; left: double serpentine; middle: serpentine on the center line.

4 Serpentines through the arena, three (light dots) and four (dark dots) curves. These can also be ridden in S-shape.

5 Volte and change of direction. Depending on the training level of the horse, the volte can be ridden in a 10-, 8-, or 6-meter diameter circle.

track. This does not really matter as long as the horse is not ridden all the time because he is—within his natural crookedness—in lateral balance (see "Straightening" on p. 161).

Under the rider, however, this natural crookedness intensifies: The horse always steps past the track of the front leg on one side. This has long-term consequences: Tendons, ligaments, and joints are stressed to a different degree and, therefore, they wear out more quickly.

Another aspect: Under the added weight of the rider, the horse must rebalance himself laterally. This can only be achieved if, during his education, you help the horse overcome this natural crookedness by proper gymnasticizing thus enabling him to develop an "artificially" straight body posture, so to speak.

This is not an end in itself but it's a necessary measure to maintain every riding horse's soundness, regardless of whether you engage in recreational riding or performance sports!

Riding curves, and later, doing lateral work, are suitable methods to overcome the natural crookedness of the horse.

The one goal that you want to achieve, therefore, is enabling the horse to find a better lateral balance by means of "straightening bending work"—via flexing and bending. Ultimately, this is only possible when the rider succeeds in aligning the inside shoulder in front of its corresponding inside hind leg (see p. 163) and—in the process—prevents the hindquarters from escaping.

Only when it is possible to flex and bend the horse correctly and thus improve his lateral balance will you be able to utilize the third basic riding technique—the half-halt—in such an effective manner that the balance of forehand and hindquarters can be created according to the degree of collection desired.

During the half-pirouette in the walk or during the turn-on-the-haunches (top image), the horse is flexed and bent into the direction of movement. Travers in the canter on the long side is a useful exercise for achieving long-term straightness.

What Does Gymnasticizing Mean?

The physical performance of rider and horse are profoundly enhanced by incorporating gymnasticizing principles. By applying the techniques listed in the sidebars above, both rider and horse will be able to more easily adjust to each changing scenario on a physical and mental level. (Remember that any type of monotony has a dulling effect on both participants, so change is necessary.)

Three Fundamental Riding Techniques

Gymnasticizing Principles for the Horse

- Changing between the gaits—walk, trot, canter—(transitions) with rhythm and suppleness.
- Changing lead (work equally on both leads).
- Transitions within the gait (change of tempo).
- "Straightening bending" work (to begin turn on the forehand, later turn on the haunches).
- Changing the horse's shape/frame (relative elevation, collection).
- Alternating between driving and carrying power.
- Working with constant consideration of suppleness and impulsion ("Schwung").
- Incorporating the surroundings for the purpose of varying the work (different footing, going uphill and downhill, tackling obstacles, for example).

A "square" halt. Only when the horse distributes his weight equally on all four feet can he instantly be motivated to move off in any desired gait.

Gymnasticizing principles for the rider

- Varying the range of motion.
- Varying speed.
- Changing levels of effort.
- Doing exercises in various positions.
- Using both sides of the body.
- Trying balance challenges: doing various physical movements with your eyes closed, for example.

When thinking about predictability, you must consider that no two riding situations are ever alike. In order to produce a continuous level of performance (with no decline in the level), it is necessary for both rider and horse to be able to quickly adjust to constantly changing events.

Conclusion: Unfortunately, the well-known gymnasticizing principles for horses, and the motion principles for flexible and stable rider movement are not sufficiently practiced. As a result, the conversation between rider and horse is not receiving "support" so the ride often proceeds in a much too stereotypical way as if following an instruction manual, rather than being individual. Subsequently, this creates physical and coordination barriers: Body and brain do not act and react quickly and flexibly enough, which impedes the ability to fully tap into any performance potential.

Flexing—The Technique

With *flexing*, the rider can pursue several different objectives. Generally, a horse must be flexed before you initiate a change in direction, for example, from the right to left lead. Furthermore, the horse must be flexed (also bent, see p. 86) when you ride a curved line such as a circle or a turn. And with an advanced horse, there is an additional aspect: In order to be able to ride the naturally crooked horse straight (or maintain straightness in flexion), it is necessary to ride the horse "with flexion" on a straight line (see p. 167).

First, however, the young, uneducated horse must learn to be ridden in flexion. To do this, you turn the horse's head just enough to be able to see—from your position on the horse's back—the inside eye and nostril. The horse's ears remain at the same level and the crest tilts into the direction in which the horse is being flexed.

Flexion only pertains to the front of the horse, meaning head, poll, and neck.

Conclusion: In most cases, flexion initiates a turn. You could also say that you never make a turn without flexing the horse first. Flexing is also prerequisite for straightening the horse.

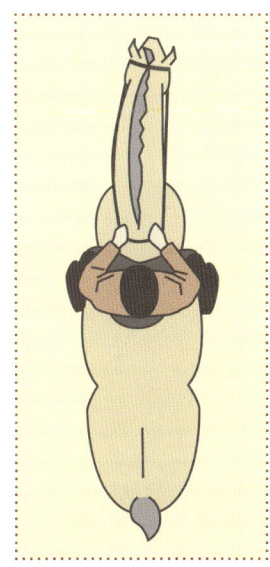

Flexion only pertains to the front of the horse, meaning the head, poll, and neck.

In canter on the left lead, the horse is flexed to the left. On the right lead, it is the other way around.

In order to initiate a turn, the horse is first flexed into the direction of the turn. Then, for the turn, the rider must shift more of her weight onto the inside seat bone.

Step-By-Step Flexion of the Horse

The basic sequence of flexing the horse can be divided into four steps:

1. **Request flexion:** You slightly shorten the inside rein. As long as flexion is only requested, your weight remains equal on both sides with your driving aids matching the gait and direction.
2. **Allow flexion:** You must now allow with the outside rein the extent of flexion you just requested with the inside rein. This means you must lengthen the outside rein to the same extent that the inside rein is shortened.
3. **Limit flexion:** The outside rein, however, also has the task of not allowing unlimited flexion—it dictates how far the horse should flex in his poll and neck.
4. **Yield with the inside rein:** According to the principle of diagonal aids (see p. 87), you now continue to guide the flexed horse on the outside rein and slightly yield with the inside rein (which had initially asked for flexion). In this situation, your inside driving leg is of special significance while your outside leg guards and drives.

Self-Monitoring

When the rider sits on a normal chair and lifts her left and right hips, she will immediately feel that this lifting is easier to do on one side than the other.

The side that is more flexible can—from the weight aid—influence the horse more actively. This carries the risk that the rider's weight is not distributed equally on both sides of the horse, so the horse becomes crooked. This, in turn, has an effect on the horse's neck carriage. For example, the horse will carry his head crooked, or torque his neck too far to the inside. This alone causes a problem with the outside hand yielding while you shorten the inside rein at the same time. Therefore, every rider should monitor herself to be sure she is equally flexible in the pelvis to the right and to the left so that both seat bones can have an identical influence.

When the rider is unable to equally influence the horse with both her seat bones, it's also difficult to hold the reins properly. If the pelvis torques when shifting weight to one side, she automatically collapses in the hip. This bend, in turn, transfers to the spine, which then slightly curves to one side. As a result, her hands may no longer be

Flexing—The Technique

By regularly exercising on a Balimo (p. 46), a rider improves pelvic flexibility. Then it's easier for her to adjust herself to the horse's back movement.

The rider on the right is only able to develop a soft and elastic way of holding the reins when she has a flexible pelvis. A movement such as counter shoulder-in requires complex movements from the rider.

positioned at the same height, which means they will influence the horse's mouth unequally with a negative effect on flexion.

The Connection Between the Pelvis and the Manner of Holding the Reins

When holding the reins, in order to maintain contact the goal is to simultaneously yield the outside hand to the same extent that the inside hand is shortening the rein. In the process, the driving influence must be maintained. This required rein aid presupposes that the rider has good control of her body and can give the rein aids independently of other body parts. Riders often give hard rein aids without intending to do so.

A precondition for being able to give soft rein aids while flexing the horse is a supple pelvis, which means the rider will be able to securely give rein aids from an independent seat. *Hand* errors are often *pelvis* errors caused by a tight shoulder or a lack of flexibility in elbow and wrist joints.

When a rider is unable to "melt into" her pelvis and the horse's back movement, her non-rhythmic pelvic movements will be

> **Incorrect Rein Aids and Their Root Causes**
>
> It is equally important for instructor and rider to find the root cause for incorrect rein aids. The reasons can be a lack of balance on the part of the rider but also insufficient flexibility in the pelvis. Another possible cause is a tight shoulder. The rider can only improve her rein aids in the long term when the reason for the problem is found.

transferred to her hands, so it is completely counterproductive to try and correct the resulting "bouncing" when holding the reins without first dealing with the lack of flexibility in her pelvis. It will no longer be possible to coordinate rein aids with sensitivity and, as a result, horses will be hard to flex since continuous contact is lost.

Only a rider who sits in balance with a flexible pelvis is able to create changes in rein length and contact in a way that will allow her to remain in the same position in the saddle. In the process, it is necessary to use the arms softly from the shoulder joints without causing any torque in your upper body because it has a negative effect on the load on each seat bone.

Problem in Shoulders and Wrists

Difficulties in flexing correctly can be caused by a lack of flexibility in the shoulder joint that leads to a lesser degree of softness in the arms. This means you cannot use your arms elastically and independently of your upper body when yielding with the outside rein. The result is faulty contact with the horse, since all movements—in spite of the rider's best efforts—will no longer occur softly and in a coordinated fashion.

Likewise, this can create difficulties when shortening the inside rein. Many riders find it difficult to turn their wrist toward the inside, so that the fingers—turned in toward the softly closed fist—move closer to the forearm.

While turning the wrist to the inside, however, it should not become fixed in a set or still position. Instead, there should be constantly finely tuned, rhythmic yielding and asking movements (hardly visible) in this turned-in position (this also applies to the outside rein).

Conclusion: As far as the coordination of aids is concerned, riders must first focus on their weight aids before discussing the manner of holding the reins more thoroughly. Furthermore, they need to be sufficiently flexible in the pelvis, the shoulders, and the wrists.

A wrong way of holding the reins can be caused by an incorrect weight aid, and also by lack of flexibility in shoulders or wrists. The rider's instructor should, therefore, diligently investigate the problem's true root cause.

Exercises

Hip Joints in All Directions (photo 1): While sitting in the saddle, move your hip joints individually forward, back, then in one connected movement. Next, perform the same movement up, down (lifting and lowering each hip joint) and as one connected movement. Finally, perform the movements clockwise and counter-clockwise (on both sides).

Head and Hip Movements: Tilt your head to the side while the hip moves toward the head (shortening); practice on both sides. This exercise can also be performed with opposite head and hip movements (see above, lifting and lowering)—head and hips move away from each other, then approach each other again.

Shoulders in All Directions (photos 2–5): Lift your shoulders, lower them, then connect lifting with lowering. Next, push your shoulders forward, then pull them back and connect the movements in both directions (practice on both sides). After that, make circular movements.

In order to gain more flexibility in her pelvis, the rider can perform various movements with the hip (lift, lower, forward, and back) while sitting on the horse.

Flex, Extend, Turn, Rotate the Wrists: Flex the wrists in both directions, supporting the flex with the other hand (a passive stretch in both directions). Turn the forearms around the ulna and radius toward the inside and the outside, then move the wrists in circular motions clockwise and counter-clockwise.

Loosening the shoulders: The rider can make circular movements with her shoulders, or lift and lower them. Many variations have a positive effect.

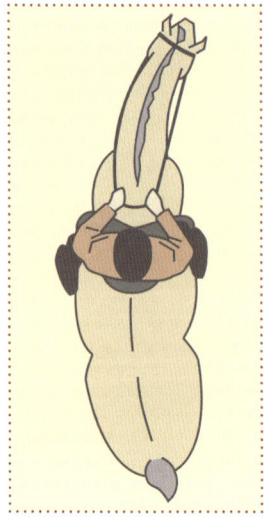

The circle is a slightly curved line. As illustrated in this drawing, the horse should be bent according to this line. If the turn was tighter—as in a volte, for example—the bend in the horse's longitudinal axis would have to be increased.

The technique of bending involves the entire longitudinal axis of the horse's body.

Bending—The Technique

In order to be able to ride a turn, the rider must not only master the technique of flexing the horse but also bending. While flexing mainly pertains to the front part of the horse's body, bending always involves the entire longitudinal axis of the horse, meaning from the head over the poll to the tail.

The extent of the bend depends on the flexibility of the horse's individual body parts. The horse's flexibility is greatest in the neck and chest area then gradually decreases to the lumbar area, which is relatively inflexible. In the area of the hindquarters—at the fused sacral vertebrae (sacrum)—it is anatomically impossible to create any bend. The tail, however, is extremely flexible (see drawing on p. 90).

Nevertheless, the Riding Theory speaks of bending the horse's body in his entire longitudinal axis. The barrel and the ribs play a

special role in bending work: Depending on the horse's conformation (ribs well sprung or not, for example), the rider on the bent horse will have the subjective perception that the arc of the horse's ribs lowers on the inside of the bend and that she is "set down" on that side of the horse. In detail, this is what happens: First, the rider influences the horse with the unilateral weight aid (that is, she shifts more weight onto one seat bone than the other) and her leg, so that the horse "hollows" and slightly lowers the arc of the ribs. Later, the rider will be able to apply the weight aid more intensely: Her inner seat bone and the inner hip joint follow the horse's movement without losing contact with the outside seat bone; the outside seat bone must still be "loaded," just not as much as the inside seat bone.

> **Bending with Flexion? It Doesn't Work!**
>
> A horse can be flexed without being bent; the other way around, however, is impossible. Remember: There is flexion without bend, but never bend without flexion.

This horse—not yet straightened—still evades bearing the load with the right hind leg. This is completely normal in horses that are naturally crooked. Shoulder-in (see photo on right) is highly suitable for straightening the horse and helps him move on a narrow track. This is being done well on the left rein.

What is the Application of Diagonal Aids?

The reasons why the rider needs so-called diagonal aids are diverse if you look at the topic in detail. However, all have one common underlying cause: the horse's anatomy.

From a trivial perspective, the fact is that the rider sits on a horse about 8 feet (2.5m) to 10 feet (3m) long, and whose longitudinal axis

> **Diagonal Aids**
>
> In equestrian sports, we speak of the "diagonal application of aids," which means the relationship between inside leg and outside rein, or outside leg and inside rein. The weight aids usually go unmentioned.

she must keep "on track" while riding. For this purpose, the rider must "frame" the horse in her aids. This is the goal of the diagonal application of aids.

At the beginning of this chapter, we mentioned the fact that the rider should influence the horse differently with her inside and outside reins in order to achieve flexion. The same applies to the weight aids, and the subsequent aids of the inside and outside leg (reminder: the weight "determines" the respective leg aid, see p. 45). In daily practical application, however, the term "diagonal aids" is only interpreted to mean leg and rein aids. The following sections will take a slightly different look at this topic:

In order to be able to create flexion and bend in the horse, the rider must understand the technique of "diagonal application of aids." This abstract term really describes a simple concept: the diagonal interplay of weight, leg, and rein aids. This means that the *inside* weight and leg aid "corresponds" to the outside rein, with the *outside* weight and leg aid, in turn, corresponding to the inside rein.

We'll use flexing to explain: When you shorten the inside rein, the outside leg must *guard* at the same time. This way, you frame the horse with your aids. Without this guarding outside leg, the horse could eventually push his hindquarters outward. At the same time, your outside rein must limit the horse's flexion. Your inside leg supports the flexion and—together with the outside leg—provides the forward movement.

When the horse is flexed in preparation for an immediate turn, the rider must let her weight aid fluidly change from a *bilateral, even* weight distribution to a predominantly *unilateral, inside* weight aid. The horse must also be slightly flexed and bent when riding in flexion, for instance, along the long side. This also requires the unilateral, inside weight aid (more on this topic on p. 44).

The principle of the diagonal application of aids—the communication between weight, leg, and rein aids—must be firmly rooted in the rider's body language. Otherwise, the consequences of incorrect application of aids will become increasingly visible as the lessons become more difficult. Examples are the horse tilts his poll, "falls out" through his outside shoulder, insufficiently develops impulsion, or has a lack of willingness to collect.

During leg-yielding, the horse always remains straight in his longitudinal axis, and he is only flexed, not bent. The photo on the left clearly shows the lateral driving leg aid with the rider's right leg. Her limiting rein aid on the left side contributes largely to the fact that the horse is not tilting in the poll.

It often goes unmentioned quite how important the correct weight aids are in connection with the application of diagonal aids, but they are of essential significance since the three-dimensionality of the movement of the horse's back corresponds with the movement of the rider's pelvis. When the three-dimensionality of the rider's pelvis is not a given, it becomes impossible to apply diagonal aids.

Bend in Ribs and Loins

The rider—in addition to proper flexion—must also ensure that the rib and loin area of the horse is bent properly. A frequently made statement is that longitudinal bend in the horse is really limited to the head, neck, and rib, meaning, we suppose that the horse is not able to bend from the lumbar vertebrae to the sacral vertebrae. However, once you observe a horse that turns when being loaded onto a trailer or is in a situation in a tight wash stall, you can see immediately how flexible the lumbar area of the horse really is. The horse can (in an emergency)

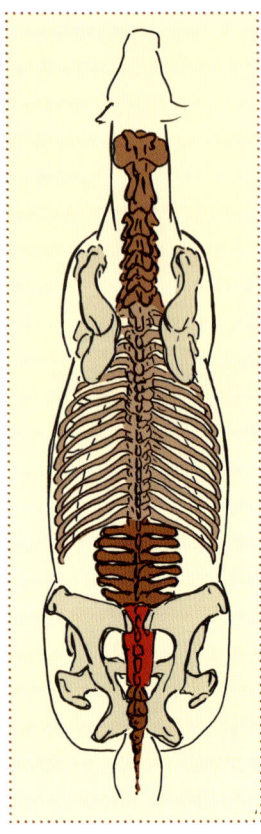

In the horse, the flexibility of vertebrae decreases gradually. You can clearly see the fused sacral vertebrae that make up the sacrum (in red). This part of the horse's spine does not bend. The tail vertebrae, however, are flexible and participate in the bend of the longitudinal axis.

use this as a sort of "articulated steering" method. This does not mean that you are looking for that extreme of a bend, but the conclusion is hugely important: The bend in the longitudinal axis does not only happen in the area of the ribs but from the poll to the tail; it is only "interrupted" at the sacrum where the sacral vertebrae are fused.

In daily practical application, we often speak of bending the horse "around the inside leg." It would be more correct, of course, to address the entire diagonal application of aids: The driving aids of the inside leg—resulting from the weight aid—must be coordinated with the outside rein, and vice versa. The rider must not fix the hand rigidly after yielding, instead, she must answer to the driving dynamics of the inside leg by making subtle, hardly visible, yielding/asking movements. This is the only way to prevent the horse from tilting in the poll.

The Inside Leg

When using the inside leg, its placement (when bending the horse it should be driving at the girth to activate the hind foot on the same side) and its rhythmic influence are important. If the inside leg is placed too far behind the girth, it hinders the bend in the rib and lumbar area. In addition, the horse's inside hind leg would then increase its upward movement instead of swinging forward with good ground coverage, as desired and the result: The horse's "engine" is inhibited and the coordination of the diagonal aids disturbed.

Rhythmic driving leads to an internal dynamic of contracting and relaxing all involved muscles, so that the horse is bent along his longitudinal axis, but continuously moving rhythmically and dynamically within this bend from the inside leg to the outside hand.

The Pelvis

During bending, the rider should shift more weight onto her inside seat bone without having her outside seat bone lose contact with the saddle and, therefore, with the horse's back. Kinematically, the rider does it correctly when she rolls her pelvis from its normal position into the direction of her left or right knee; depending on the schooling level of the horse and the desired lesson, she is, therefore, able to create different levels of bend (lessons start on p. 170). Consequently, the rider's

Bending—The Technique

In order to bend the horse to the left, the rider must roll her pelvis from its normal position into the direction of her left knee. The rider on the left shows how the rolling pelvis supports the bend in the horse. On the right, however, horse and rider stay mostly straight.

movement stays "in the horse," the horse is able to step underneath his center of gravity, and his balance is not disturbed by the rider pushing her pelvis forward, torquing it, or by collapsing in the hip.

The Outside Leg

From a loosely hanging thigh, the "guarding" outside leg must be positioned back from the knee joint without difficulty, and without clamping, either. Nowadays, however, many riders are blocked in the hip joints due to the fact that their hip joint is not fully utilized in its function as a ball joint, but as a hinge joint. The result is a lack of flexibility in the pelvis. When the rider is supposed to bring her outside leg back, she often does this by moving the entire leg back, instead of it being an easy movement from the knee joint. This movement of the entire leg leads to a blockage and torquing of the pelvis, which has a negative effect on the longitudinal bend of the horse. An incorrect shift in the rider's pelvis has an effect on the continuous flow of the horse's longitudinal bend.

The exercises from the Six-Point Program (hip joint in all directions, see pp. 35 and 42) are suitable for achieving good flexibility in the hip. Next to flexibility in the hip joint, it is also important to have a flexible knee joint. You can often observe that the ability to flex is not optimal and a rider is also unable to just let the leg hang down. With these riders, the hamstrings are very "stressed." They can be made more flexible through stimulation from your fingers. After this exercise, riders are mostly able to use the leg with sensitivity for driving and then relax it afterward.

Exercise

For the Knee Joints: Sit comfortably on a chair so that thigh and lower leg just about form a 90-degree angle. Use your fingers to grasp your thigh in the junction between thigh and knee. On the right and left, under the knee, you can feel tendons. "Pluck" them several times.

This rider is "plucking" the tendons underneath the knee.

Manner of Holding the Reins

We have already discussed in detail the manner of holding the reins in the section about the technique of flexing (p. 83), whereby the movements during bending must be performed with even greater coordination. A greater deviation to the outside or inside would have an even stronger negative effect in the longitudinal bend than during flexion.

Good coordination between the outside and inside rein is the prerequisite for not having the horse fall out with his outside shoulder by creating too strong a neck angle.

Coordination of weight, leg, and rein aids for bending requires the rider to have highly developed proprioception. If the rider, for example, wants to ride a turn to the left, she first flexes the horse to the left then bends him to the left, and she must initiate a unilateral weight aid on the left side. In the process, her oblique muscles must function in such a way as to prevent her outside shoulder from falling back during her weight shift. When the obliques do not function and the outside shoulder falls back, there are issues with her ability to hold the reins properly—an automatic reaction causes the rider to pull the outside rein back. This series of events can cause the entire interplay to fail, since during a turn, the outside rein must act forward, not backward.

Bending—The Technique

During turns, the rider must have cross-coordination control over her body: Her shoulder follows the horse's shoulder and her hip follows that of the horse.

It is important for the rider that her body has functional cross coordination in order to perform the interplay of the weight shift and manner of holding the reins without having to think about it, so that the horse can move naturally in accordance with his own system.

Exercise
Crossover Movements on the Longe Line: Turn your eyes in the opposite direction of the shoulders; turn the head in the opposite direction of the shoulders; turn your shoulders in the opposite direction to the hips; turn your stretched-out arms in the opposite direction to your head; turn your arms in the opposite direction to the hips; twist in monkey position: left hand touches the right toes and vice versa; have your knee touch the opposite elbow.

Half-Halts—The Technique

"Half-halt" is the term that describes a finely coordinated interplay of weight, leg, and rein aids. The half-halt is a method to change gait, tempo, and the horse's shape (degree of collection). Furthermore, during the horse's ongoing schooling, the half-halt serves to ensure the horse's ability to shift the balance point from his forehand toward the hindquarters (and, therefore, his ability to be collected). This is the goal that the rider strives for during the horse's schooling. She can only achieve it when she is able to apply the fundamental riding technique of high-quality half-halts. Therefore, the half-halt virtually plays the "key role" in the horse's schooling: Only the application of half-halts makes advanced schooling (and, therefore, increased performance) altogether possible.

First of all, however, the horse requires a certain amount of basic training in order to be able to entirely implement the operating principle of the half-halt. Among other things, it must be possible to be able to ask for a small amount of flexion and bend from the horse, and the horse must already have begun to straighten.

Nevertheless, half-halts are incorporated into more or less every movement of the horse under the rider, right from the beginning of the horse's schooling. This applies to changes of direction and changes of speed—even if the quality will not be the same as it will be at an advanced schooling level. Once again, this circumstance illustrates how important it is that one of the two beings that carry on this riding conversation have a developmental edge: either the rider or the horse. Due to the fact that she masters the half-halt technique, an experienced rider is able to make the young horse understand from the start that there is an interplay between all aids.

The term "half-halt" is an equestrian definition that causes much confusion, especially for inexperienced riders. Many interpret it to merely be the rein aid part of it. This is wrong. A half-halt is always a synergy of all three aids available to the rider, even though the driving aids are the predominant ones.

In order to be able to correctly carry out half-halts, it is absolutely necessary to be on a schooled horse so the rider can learn to "feel" the process: when to drive, when to keep the hands still, and when to

The horse needs a certain amount of schooling in order for the rider to be able to apply the half-halt technique effectively.

push the hands forward a bit. It is almost impossible to teach a rider how riding with half-halts works just by giving rational instructions. It is, rather, a matter of constant practice and trial and error, whereby an outside observer can give the rider feedback while she carries out the technique with sensitivity (ideas for an effective dialogue between instructor and riding student can be found on p. 117). Furthermore, it makes sense to first try the interplay between aids on the longe line, then later, during free riding.

Conclusion: The interplay of aids must be very exact so that you can achieve the desired effect in the horse at the moment of the half-halt, meaning the change in gait, tempo, or shape. This concept is not new. The book *The Rider Forms the Horse* (First Edition, 1939) points out that only by means of half-halts—described in the exact same way—can the rider develop the so-called "flexion of the haunches" (see collection on p. 176) and that it is impossible to create high-quality collection without the application of half-halts.

What Does the Rider "Feel" When She Should Apply a Half-Halt?

It is always a risky undertaking to try and describe "feel." Just as it is impossible to dispute matters of taste, each rider would probably describe her riding "feel" a bit differently when she applies a half-halt. An attempt to describe the feel could be something like this: The horse determines the right moment, which is when all of the horse's joints are flexing during movement. This is when the rider "gathers" the horse's impulsion into a slightly more closed body frame (shape). To explain further, the horse flexes his large joints from the hip through the stifle to the hock, and farther on down. Thus, his pelvis is tilted, his croup lowers, and his muscles cause his back to arch slightly upward. As a prerequisite, the rider needs to be very supple on the horse's back since her pelvis must "receive" the movement of the horse's arching back and follow it, meaning she slightly tilts backward and her pelvis gets "sucked" into the horse's back movement. As a result, she will feel how her lower leg softly and automatically "clings" to the horse's body, since her backward-tilted pelvis initiates the driving impulse in her lower leg. At the same time, her hands follow the movement of her pelvis.

> **Half-Halts**
> In equestrian sports, half-halts have played a key role since they allow the rider to influence the horse's gait, tempo, and shape. Only when this is successfully accomplished is it possible to achieve constant improvement in performance.

During the moment of suspension in the horse's trot or canter, the rider's pelvis tilts slightly forward again, and as a result, her lower leg somewhat disconnects from the horse's body and her hands move slightly and elastically forward. This is the moment when the rider "lets the horse's forward impulsion out." When the horse's hooves make contact with the ground and the joints flex once more (see impulsion on p. 148), the rider can utilize the next half-halt in the rhythm that is predetermined by the horse. This way, the rider can influence the horse with many consecutive half-halts that accompany the horse's every movement—sometimes more, sometimes less

During every one of the horse's movements the rider has the opportunity to influence the horse through half-halts.

pronounced. The functional principle is similar to a perpetual motion machine, since all of the horse's movements, whether at the walk, trot, or canter, give the rider the recurring opportunity to use the half-halt technique to influence the horse.

Since describing how and to what extent half-halts are applied is so complex, consider this thought: "The horse 'collects' the half-halt from the rider." This means that through the rhythm and sequence of his movement, the horse determines how and to what extent the rider applies the half-halt; however, this should not mean that the half-halt is ridden in a *reactive* manner: Being able to *actively* utilize the half-halt requires a great deal of coordination on part of the rider.

The following example is a fitting comparison: Take a ball and keep bouncing it on the floor with one hand. When the ball jumps up toward your hand, you first receive the ball's movement, meaning you act *reactively*. Then, however, you can influence the ball's direction and dynamics by lifting and lowering your wrist. You are, therefore using your own activity to bring energy into the "conversation" between a human hand and the ball. Just like when bouncing a ball, the rider must use her proprioception and skills in order to find the correct moment for the half-halt. Those who have developed proprioception during their riding education can "feel" the point in time when they must collect the horse's impulsion, retain it, then with a yielding rein aid, immediately allow the horse to swing forward.

Conclusion: Half-halts can only be used effectively when the principles of flexing and bending can be applied. They are used to influence gait, tempo, and the shape of the horse and are necessary when riding any kind of transitions. (In order to feel the correct moment to apply the half-halt aids, the rider must have a well-developed sense of proprioception.)

Coordination of Aids During Half-Halts

The rider must be prepared to coordinate her aids during the half-halt, a big test of her riding skills and coordination. But she cannot learn this simply by "being moved" passively ("reacting" rather than "acting") on a schoolmaster. Furthermore, since there are no comparable skills that a rider can fall back on that would allow her to transfer the

It is not possible to achieve the full effectiveness of half-halts with a young horse, unless you are an experienced rider who can apply the sequences of the half-halt from the beginning and during the course of schooling with the result that the horse will increasingly be affected by them.

skill to riding, this transfer must occur by using a rider's various abilities (see p. 17).

Just as it is part of training for other sports, the rider should be able to fulfill intricate, complex tasks, which must occur simultaneously, consecutively, and under time pressure. As a consequence the rider becomes more sensitive to her coordination abilities. She can then *act* and *react* during situational changes without any difficulty.

Various cross-coordination exercises turning around the longitudinal axis provide the best preparation since they involve using both sides of the body via the brain. Since all riding situations must constantly occur in the so-called "spiral" seat, these exercises assist with the interplay of aids—especially across the diagonals of our body (see "diagonal application of aids" on p. 87).

Half-Halts—The Technique

Exercises

Warm-Up Exercises: The rider fulfills tasks that call for various sequences at the same time, for example:
- Walking and circling one arm
- Walking and circling both arms consecutively—like a windmill—from front to back, and vice versa
- Walking and circling both arms at the same time from front to back, and vice versa
- Skipping and circling both arms from back to front, and vice versa

These circling exercises must be carried out slowly.

Exercises on the Balance Trainer with a Ball:
- Stand on both legs and throw the ball from left to right (1).
- Stand on one leg and throw the ball up in the air (2).

All these exercises can help the rider increasingly become better able to fine-tune her aids and her influence while applying the half-halt.

The goal is for the rider not only to reactively experience the half-halt, but to be able to actively use it in order to change, for example, the gait, movement sequence, and posture of the horse. Nowhere does the desired conversation between rider and horse become more clearly apparent than in the skillful application of half-halts.

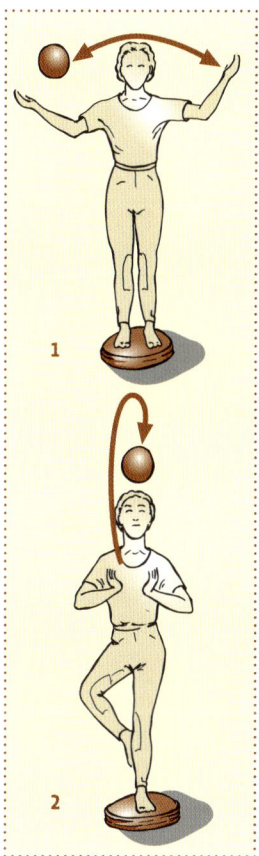

Movement requirements that link various tasks (in combination) during exercises without the horse help the rider to learn the half-halt.

At a Glance

- Flexing and bending demand complex movements from the rider. The goal is to be able to apply diagonal aids.
- Half-halting serves to change the gait, tempo, and posture of the horse.
- The rider needs a well-developed and fine-tuned sense of proprioception to be able to find the correct moment for the application of the half-halt.
- Various tasks from the science of biomechanics can help the rider to improve her coordination abilities so she can more easily ride consecutive half-halts.

Learning How to Ride in Conversation

Functional Riding Instruction

Unfortunately, today, many riding facilities teach lessons in a specific order while the reasons for this format and the active principles behind the lessons are no longer explained in detail; in other words, teaching is formalized and is not *functional* instruction. For example, many a rider only learns that at the beginning of the riding session, you go large (around the entire perimeter of the arena) and ride circles, then turns-on-the-forehand and leg-yielding, later voltes and serpentines. The reason "why," however, is usually not provided.

Below, we will provide various examples for conducting logical and meaningful riding lessons.

Riding Lesson Format According to Sports Education Principles

A prerequisite for what is going to happen during the riding lesson is the analysis of rider and horse. Usually, though, an instructor will ask the rider to execute various lessons that are listed in *Riding Theory*. Instead, the selection of lesson content (see p. 107) and their goals should have been exclusively selected as result of the preceding thorough analysis of rider and horse.

The instructor's demands on a riding student should be closely related to the previously gained competencies of rider and horse in order to ensure successful instruction (i.e. with no excessive demands). The less the difference is between what is currently asked for and what has been already achieved, the more likely it is that rider and horse will experience success.

The respective Training Scales apply to the rider as well as to the horse and serve as the relevant guidelines for the analysis of the actual state of rider and horse. Likewise, the selection of riding lessons according to methodical steps should always be guided by the Training Scales for rider and horse.

Variables that influence decisions are current performance level, physical characteristics, conformation, and psychological qualities of rider and horse.

In order to make riding instruction effective, it must be preceded by an analysis of rider and horse.

An analysis should include looking at the rider from various different angles.

Example of an Analysis

The performance level of the rider is Novice: She has a relaxed frame of mind but there is some lack of suppleness in the shoulder area. In the pelvis, however, the rider is flexible. This somewhat makes up for her partially tense neck/shoulder area, since she is largely able to sit in the center of gravity and rhythm of the horse due to her flexibility in the pelvis. The rider is able to demonstrate the skills required at First Level. She would be able to execute these lessons with more exact coordination if the weakness in her upper body was reduced. This weakness has been having a negative effect on the fine-tuning of her rein aids.

Her horse has securely mastered the lessons of First and Second Level, and is therefore a suitable schoolmaster for the rider. The fact that the horse is secure somewhat makes up for the weakness in the rider's upper body. Due to his own security, the horse is able to largely transfer his feeling for balance and rhythm to the rider in a positive manner. The rider can, therefore, experience proprioception that is externally supported by the horse.

The horse's conformation is harmonious and without considerable weaknesses. Due to his even-tempered disposition, he is especially suited to be a schoolmaster. The activity of his hindquarters could be improved if the rider were able to fine-tune her rein aids.

Lesson Contents

The sequence of the lesson—contents, objective, topic, goal, method (sequence of steps), and evaluation (to be assessed later)—is decided as a result of the analysis already done, and will only work when the ability of rider and horse forms a starting point for current—and future—instruction.

The terminology of lesson planning is not identical to the terminology of the Riding Theory, so it might initially sound confusing when we choose to use the word "contents" for "lessons" (i.e. skills and technique). Not only are skills part of the "contents" or the topic of instruction, but also coordination abilities (e. g. coordination of aids).

An Everyday Riding Situation

In everyday life, the rider often asks the instructor what she will be riding in today's lesson. The response is usually something like:

"Today, you will ride serpentines, or flying-lead changes, or...." and the instructor's response is limited to listing various school figures. But lessons should not be simply about skills where the horse—due to the rider's aids and influence—displays a certain form and appearance, but should also consists of exercises with a purpose—ones that should be designed differently according to each individual horse. Therefore, it is not all about *form* but about *function*, too, so the horse can be schooled according to his natural ability—thus remaining sound for a long time.

Every lesson incorporates several functions that riders and instructors must take into account. For this reason, let's clarify the basic structure of the instructor's planning process.

The Planning Process

When structuring a lesson plan (after analyzing horse and rider) the instructor must basically decide between the following aspects: Content, Topic, Objective, Method, and Evaluation.

In this context, the teacher must also consider the reciprocal effects between content and method, that is, reflect on the content, topic, and goal before deciding on the method.

First, we need to determine what content means in the context of riding. Initially, contents are "neutral" since they can be used for various riding purposes: They are specific movements, such as serpentines, backing up, or counter-canter, for example. It is not worth riding them and striving for form if you do not also have objectives in mind that specifically relate to your horse.

Example: Riding Serpentines
Content: Serpentines
Topic: Development of various serpentines with a special consideration toward fine-tuning the rein aids during changes in the horse's tempo.
Objective: First, as a prerequisite for soft contact with the horse's mouth the rider performs exercises for the mobilization of the shoulder joints (p. 40). These will improve the coordination

---

Planning a Riding Lesson
Successfully planning a riding lesson includes various aspects. First, the topic of the lesson is defined and formulated, then the method. After the lesson, an assessment will help to draw conclusions as to how to proceed.

During a riding lesson, the rider may become overwhelmed, depending on which method (series of steps) was selected. In the photo on the left, for example, the rider is not yet able to ride a serpentine, so the instructor must select different steps until the exercise is either visibly improved or mostly successful (photo on right).

between inside and outside rein aids when riding frequent changes in direction in serpentines. By riding the serpentine, the horse should gain suppleness in his longitudinal axis, and his hindquarters are encouraged to step on a narrow track.

Method:
- Riding a circle at the trot
- Change of rein from circle to circle
- Simple serpentine on the long side alternating with lengthening of stride on the long side
- Serpentines through the arena (S-shape)
- Then, again, lengthening of stride

Evaluation: The rider is not yet able to demonstrate that she can continuously hold the reins in a way that the lessons ask from her. She still tends to put too much emphasis on the "asking" rein aid, so a finely coordinated contact of the rein aids remains to be developed. For this purpose, it is necessary to have the rider perform additional specific exercises for the arm/shoulder area before riding. Before working on additional serpentines, she should practice frequent changes of direction on the circle. Only when these are successfully executed with finely coordinated rein aids should the rider resume working with serpentines.

Some Additional Topics
- Backing in order to check the horse's suppleness.
- Transitions and riding on a curved line in order to improve the coordination of rider aids.
- Counter-canter for the purpose of straightening the horse.

Suggested topics and objectives can pertain to the horse and/or rider. The instructor should be specific about what is to be achieved from each exercise, otherwise, there is the risk that the riding lesson will turn into a string of exercises whereby the rider is unable to discern what the actual goal is.

> **Checking Goals**
> As they pertain to riding, goals are changes in behavior in horses and riders, whereby criteria (in this case, quality of movement sequences) must be specified when mapping out the goals. Effectiveness of instruction can only be evaluated by using these criteria.

A Methodical Approach
After mapping out the topic and goal, the *method* is addressed. Here is an example.

Method (Exercise sequences):
- Transitions. Collected trot/working trot on the circle; first on the left rein, then change of rein through the circle at a collected tempo,
- Transitions. Collected canter/working canter on the circle; first on the right rein, transition down to a collected trot then change of rein through the circle,
- Tighten and enlarge the circle on the left rein, then go large, ride a volte in the center of the long side or in the second corner of the short side,
- Shoulder-in to the center of the long side, then straighten, increase tempo for a few strides, then collect,

- Before the short side, collected tempo,
- Shoulder-in on the long side.

Instruction

The type of instruction should be as little *instructor*-oriented and as much *task*-oriented as possible. This enables an exchange between rider and instructor (see suggestions for dialog during riding instruction on p. 117).

The sequence of school figures and exercises are less important than the reason why the instructor has chosen a specific exercise—in coordination with the rider.

In other words, the topic chosen by the instructor depends on what the goal is and which method (exercise steps) should be used to reach the goal.

It is possible, for example, to ride trot/canter transitions as *suppling* transitions. It is equally possible, however, to ride these same transitions on curved lines in a way that emphasizes the development of *impulsion*.

In the system of the Riding Theory, it does not make sense to imperatively assign each known exercise to a specific phase of the riding session, according to the motto: Trot/canter transitions are only suitable for suppling work, whereas voltes and serpentines are only for straightening the horse.

Almost any exercise available to the rider can be varied in its execution and therefore be applied for different goals. So in order to give a riding lesson an individual structure that is tailored to the needs of horse and rider, the instructor should not necessarily follow a particular exercise sequence just because that was the way he planned it.

Instead, it is important to design instructional activity that is able to be varied in ways that correspond to the behavior of rider and horse in different situations. In the process, various aspects should be considered against the background of the Riding Theory, which are listed in the following.

Exercises with Purpose

Most exercises should not be assigned to a specific phase of a riding session, but rather to a specific function, which can vary.

Instruction against the Background of the *Riding Theory*

What Goals Are at Stake?

The following maxim applies to the operating principles of a lesson: "From elementary to difficult." So, practically, the following principles would apply:

1. An exercise that is ridden on a straight line should create an effect, for example: trot/canter transitions. The intended effect from riding a transition on a straight line is to supple the horse.

2. When the same exercise is then ridden on large, curved lines, it no longer only has suppling qualities, but adds another function: It now also acquires straightening qualities.

3. Whatever works on a *large* curved line, can be amplified on a *small* curved line. Trot/canter transitions, for instance, can be first ridden on a circle then later on a smaller curved line, for instance from a

A transition on a straight line has mostly suppling qualities (left), but riding the transition on a large curved line makes this not only a suppling, but also a straightening exercise.

volte. Making the curved line smaller adds additional aspects: The horse must now be flexed and bent more, which also improves the straightening work. In addition, the tighter the turn, the more challenging it becomes for the horse to maintain his balance while executing the exercises.

4. Tightening then enlarging curved lines in spiral form presents an additional increase in difficulty.

5. You can achieve even more by riding changes of direction and tempo within the tighter curved lines. This helps achieve various goals: improved straightening, development of impulsion through tempo variation, development of carrying power by means of transitions.

By means of frequent changes in the length of stride (here from the working trot to the collected trot) the rider can pursue various goals: improved development of driving power, development of carrying power, and improved self-carriage of the horse.

Choosing the Gait

In principle, the rider has the opportunity to assign completely different goals to an exercise by choosing a specific gait. As a first step, it makes sense—especially for a beginner—to first try a movement on a standing horse, the to solidify on a moving horse. One example is "driving," to prompt the horse to move off.

Instructors view the *walk* as an "instructive" gait that is well suited to illustrate new movement sequences to the horse, for instance, crossing over with front or hind limbs during leg-yielding. At the same time, the walk is an instructive gait for the beginner rider: Based on the slowness of the gait, she has an opportunity to familiarize herself with a new sequence of moves.

Ridden at the *trot*, the same exercises, therefore, solidify the goals of achieving a higher learning or training effect for horse or rider. The trot is also called the predominant working gait since its regulated two beats with a suspension phase makes it easier for the horse to find his way through the exercises.

In *canter* work, the special characteristics of canter on the left or right lead as well as a distinct suspension phase are added to the equation. Even though it is often easier for the rider to sit the canter rather than the trot, working in this gait makes higher demands on the coordination abilities of both rider and horse.

The Objective of Turns

Within a riding session as well as during the horse's early schooling the goal is to first develop rhythm, suppleness, and contact. Later you develop driving and carrying power by focusing on impulsion, straightening, and collection.

In the early schooling phase, all exercises and turns are geared toward turns-on-the-forehand. One could say: "Turn around the forehand while riding forward." Obviously, this is most visibly illustrated in the turn-on-the-forehand exercise itself during which the horse's hind legs step in a semicircle around the forehand. But leg-yielding and large curved lines also focus more on the forehand than on the hindquarters during the early stages of schooling.

If you relate this to the dressage levels, you'll see it is reflected in the First Level requirements, which ask for "beginning" straightening, though a certain level of crookedness can be tolerated. Within the framework of a horse's overall education this usually means you should arrive at First Level after about one year of schooling.

After this, as you reach a critical turning point in schooling, the principle of turning is "turned around," so to speak. During subsequent work (starting with Second Level), the horse no longer performs turn-on-the-forehand, but instead, turn around the haunches—best seen in the key exercise half-pirouette in the walk, but also in lateral gaits up to pirouettes in the canter. (You can read more about these starting on p. 171.)

The turn-on-the-forehand is a suppling exercise, and especially suited for beginners learning about the principles of the diagonal application of aids.

Diagram for structuring a riding lesson

Name of instructor

Date/time

Place/materials

Topic of riding lesson

Preconditions (rider/horse analysis, reason for choice of topic, and learning goal)

1	2	3	4	5
No	Sequence of lesson/exercise	Description of exercise	Focus/sub-goals	Possible errors/correction
1.				
2.				
3.				
4.				

Considerations for the next lesson:

Goals Principle: Task-Oriented Instead of Instruction-Oriented

To start, the above described operating principles were listed for basic dressage schooling in the arena. This education, however, can be expanded by one critical aspect that is neglected by many riders today: the all-around, variety of basic schooling. So, in order to enable a horse to tap into his full potential, the rider should not only internalize the goals for riding on a rectangle, but also keep them in focus while riding over cavalletti, jumping, riding cross country, and during work on the longe or double-longe line.

While planning the course of a lesson, the instructor lists the individual steps of the exercises, and discusses the respective goals. Relevant suggestions toward conversational riding (see page 117) cannot be written down since the plan would otherwise consist of several pages. The riding instructor should offer the exercises in a more task-oriented versus an instruction-oriented manner. This means that he reduces the movement criteria and includes visual aids like poles and cones (see "Task-Oriented Instruction" on p. 123).

Instruction specifies all details of movement criteria in each ridden exercise. The rider does not have any leeway; she must execute movements according to the specifications. Within the ridden exercises, however, many aspects occur at the same time: For example, in canter you apply half-halts, flex the horse to the inside, use the inside leg at the girth to drive, use the outside leg one hand-width behind the girth to guard, and yield with the inside hand. The rider is being overwhelmed, though neither she nor the instructor notices it at the time.

In contrast, when giving the rider a task, the instructor provides the framework for it: For example, he asks the rider to canter on the outside track, and outlines the aids. The instructor leaves it up to the rider as to when and where she transitions into the canter, and he doesn't immediately step in after the first effort but instead gives the rider the chance to evaluate the sequence herself. This can be followed by additional steps (see "Task-Oriented Instruction" on p. 123).

Diagram Explanation
Column 1: *Consecutive numbering of the individual steps of the method*
Column 2: *Exercises that should be ridden methodically—one after another*
Column 3: *Description of exercises explaining how to ride them*
Column 4: *Each exercise contains its own goal-oriented focus points, which must be achieved on the path to the learning goal of the overall unit. Planning a riding lesson is first of all an assumption as to how the instruction would be conducted under normal conditions. Unexpected circumstances, however, can arise at any time, and these must be immediately addressed by the instructor.*
Column 5: *This is where errors and corrections are listed so the instructor can address them during the lesson.*
After the riding lesson, the instructor should discuss the course of the lesson and the goals achieved in order to present the student with a plan of work to do at home, and/or address what the specific focus of the next lesson will be.

Communication in Riding Instruction

In previous chapters, we explained which abilities and skills a rider must bring to the table—or learn—in order to conduct a successful conversation with the horse. In order to create a more intense dialogue between rider and horse, it is necessary to change the way riding instructor and riding student communicate. To illustrate this, we will briefly explain which learning styles are predominantly applied in most sports and why it is necessary to find new ways in equestrian sports.

Different Learning Styles

The way of teaching sports varies widely. In the past, it was believed that the teacher should demonstrate everything, meaning he would provide a visual explanation so the student could get an idea of the movement. This was supposed to be the basis for the student's own movement.

Later on in teaching, it becomes more common for the student not to be led exclusively by the instructor's example, that is, not to expose her to the image of only one individual instructor. Even though the demonstration would show the student how a movement looked, she couldn't easily imitate it because she can't "feel" the instructor's individual "inner" way of riding it.

There is also the issue that an instructor, due to his age, can become limited in his ability to demonstrate a movement. Consequently, he has to rely on conveying knowledge through language alone, that is, talking the student through it.

Problems When Demonstrating an Exercise

A riding lesson is only meaningful if the student has already mastered the basics of that lesson. Otherwise, the rider only recognizes the "external" form of a movement, not the dynamic correlation. But, when a rider is somewhat familiar with a movement she may find she has an automatic compulsion to follow the movement "internally" as she rides it. This effect was called the "Carpenter effect"; today it is called the "ideomotor phenomenon" (p. 69).

This insight leads to the conclusion that it is not really possible to teach new riding movements with the demonstration-and-copy

---

The "Inner" Image

Riding instruction is mainly conveyed by means of language. However, using this method, it is only possible to a limited extent to create an "inner" image of an exercise, which is necessary for the student to internalize new movement sequences.

The instructor has several ways of conveying content to his student (language, body language, image sequences, video, etc.)

method. It also does not fit into the *conversational* riding concept since—in following this system—both rider and horse must enter into a communicative process by *sensing* and *moving* each other. When the rider does not already know the movement that she is watching being demonstrated, she cannot possibly "internally" feel it, so will not develop an "inner" image; in fact, she is only receiving a superficial, "external" blueprint of the movement without being able to feel its "internal" correlation. Furthermore, the demonstrated form of the movement is an *individual* one, which cannot be performed by another person in the same way.

For every movement, each rider and each horse only have *their own* optimal movement sequence; copying a demonstrated movement would mean they erase any *individual* movement possibilities; in a way, they are just adhering to a specified form of the movement, and such adherence does not comply with the concept of conversational riding.

Conclusion: The "first demonstrate, then copy" method of teaching only makes sense when the rider already knows the basics of the exercise she is watching.

Learning through Photo Sequences

Learning movements with the help of photos with an explanatory text has the goal of presenting the visual specifications to the rider as precisely as possible. On the one hand, photos can be more exact in their detail than a live demonstration. On the other hand, photos lack the reality of dynamics, and it is dynamics that have such an important function in developing the rider/horse partnership.

Looking at, and talking about, photo sequences can make it easier to learn new lessons.

Learning with DVDs

Photos have the advantage of providing the rider with a method of *thinking* her way into an exercise sequence according to her own learning speed. But, as just mentioned, a photo sequence lacks movement. However, this problem is overcome by watching a DVD. Even though DVDs shown at their original speed may be too fast at the beginning of the learning process, in order to intuitively imagine yourself in a situation you can select slow motion or watch the sequence one image at a time; even though the movement would be a bit distorted you can restore it by playing the DVD at its normal speed afterward. Overall, contemporary human beings—due to a societal change in the way information is now available—are visual or integrative learners so that a learning medium containing "moving images" can be of great help to riders. (See *Movement Awareness for Riders* the DVD and *Rider Fitness: Body & Brain* the book by Eckart Meyners.)

Learning Through Language

In equestrian sport, teaching is mainly done through language. Most riders only learn "acoustically." Maybe this is the reason why few riders make any headway—even over the course of many years. They don't improve their "feel" and cannot conduct a conversation with their horse.

The problem when being taught via language is that everybody has a different learning style. According to her own development, a person learns with different "information" channels, whether eyes, ears, or kinesthetic (muscle sensation), and has become used to it.

There is a difference, for example, between visual, auditory, and kinesthetic learners. Conveying knowledge through words only serves the auditory learner; others have to try much harder in order to obtain relevant information about learning to ride. This already creates a barrier to "feeling yourself into" a movement (i.e. conducting a conversation with the horse).

An instructor who uses vivid descriptions and demonstrates by means of body language can help the student imagine movement sequences in her mind's eye.

Furthermore, not every riding instructor is equally competent when talking to the student. A rider is very fortunate to find a riding instructor who—based on his linguistic sensibilities—is able to explain movements more precisely, descriptively, and with more sensitivity than others.

Limits of Conveying Knowledge through Language

Language is limited in regard to the extent in which it is able to capture and express a motion sequence. Using words, an instructor can only formulate the parts of a movement consecutively, even if the parts happen at the same time. In these situations, workarounds can be used: "You must sit on the inside and at the same time…"; "…while shortening the reins, you must simultaneously….the horse from behind…." The inadequacy of language is the first obstacle that prevents development of kinesthesia (awareness of the body's position and movement via sensory organs of muscles and joints).

An additional problem is found when expressing dynamic moments; requests such as "Shorten the reins more softly" or "Yield with the reins" have a different meaning to every rider.

It is generally difficult to describe the inner-movement sequences in language, or to phrase them in a way that enables the rider to further fine-tune her aids.

Language in general is limited when it comes to conveying riding instruction. How is the instructor supposed to translate the *feel* that a rider is supposed to perceive "internally"? In most cases, the instructor formulates his own kinesthesia for the exercise. However, this is usually a hard task for the student since the instructor is much better schooled than she is; the beginner is unable to follow such requirements while riding in conversation.

Unfortunately, riding instructors are still taught to focus too much on *instruction-oriented* teaching. In this type of lesson, a rider is often assailed with an excessive amount of teaching. During the moment of learning something new, a rider can only consciously implement one movement, even though several additional new movement details will follow. Such type of instruction is more of a hindrance than a help since the large amount of instructions distract the rider from *feeling*.

Instruction and Task

Instruction-oriented lessons overtax the riding student. She is expected to implement a number of movement criteria all at the same time. In task-oriented instruction the rider has the opportunity to "feel" movement sequences and, therefore, start a conversation with the horse.

Methods to Improve Perception

If you understand riding to be a conversation between rider and horse, then the lessons must be designed based on task-oriented methods.

The difference between instruction and a task is that the instruction predetermines the exact way a movement should be carried out by the rider, while the task allows for some leeway in which the rider can develop her own solutions. At the same time, communication between instructor and rider must determine the movement criteria needed to make the riding lesson successful. Riding movements should not be carried out completely incorrectly, create a dangerous situation, or confuse the horse by presenting conflicting movements. Perception must be at the center of instruction since this is the basis for carrying on a conversation with the horse. Only when a rider feels the horse's real movement, can she react to it accordingly. Therefore, an instructor must consider the following methods, principles, and tips.

Tips for Conversational Instruction
Reduce the Number of Predetermined Movement Criteria

Instruction-oriented lessons confirm to the rider that she is unable to implement the instructor's constant correcting analyses and instructions in a way that influences the horse properly. The rider should not, for example, strive to "copy" the form of the typical, ideal riding seat. Instead, the instructor should be creative using tools at hand to help the rider experience the correct seat.

Especially with beginners, the instructor should present the rider with tasks instead of giving instruction. This gives the student the opportunity to try out the aids and feel the effect in order to make changes.

Overall, the riding instructor needs to give more thought to the question of how a rider can ride more correctly with helpful concepts, without overwhelming her with a multitude of movement parameters. For example, how many times does a jumper land on the wrong lead? The instructor emphasizes that the rider should put more weight on the stirrup on that respective side, however, we have discovered that this advice does not lead to success. Instead, if the instructor explains to the rider that while she is going over the jump she should start looking toward the next jump and the route ahead, the horse is more likely to land correctly since the rider's body movement is guided by her eye.

Offering Visual Stimuli to Create "Internal" Images

When using objects as an aid—such as cones for riding serpentines—the rider is more likely to develop better images than when she is receiving an entire set of aids from the instructor, which cause her to ride with a *conscious* effort, overthink everything, and tense too many muscles that are not needed for tackling the exercise. She, therefore, never starts to develop *feel*, and her movement and the horse's understanding of it never mesh; they fail to become a "riding unit."

The visual stimulus of the cones alone can reduce the complexity of the situation. The rider herself can recognize mistakes and can—if her own corrections are not successful—use the riding instructor's advice more quickly to realize the connection between her perception of the situation and her movement (influencing the horse) as a consequence of what happened in that particular situation.

Using Situations to Have the Rider Experience Movement Corrections

Not every rider is able to immediately translate an instructor's corrections into movement. It is more productive—and in the sense of the connection between movement and perception (conducting a conversation with the horse) more effective—to create situations that can be experienced.

This enables the rider to independently explore (feel her way through) the movement tasks in these situations. Consequently, she will develop essential movement experiences and insights by dealing with the situation.

In the process, the rider bypasses the direct path to the desired form of the exercise. The method is also called "learning intentions" whereby the intention is the realization of a desired outcome.

This intention is only conveyed to the rider in form of an overall image. For example, she is asked to ride a circle, and she must find her own personal movement pattern in order to do this. The instructor can use cones or a line drawn on the arena floor (also possibly demonstrate it himself, or show a video) to define the horse's path.

He can discuss core criteria with the student as to how she should approach this task and after that, the student attempts to tackle it for the first time.

Communication in Riding Instruction

Correct recognition of the relationship between the circumstances (situation), the rider's actions, and the horse's response: At the end of the suppling phase, the rider checks his work by letting the horse chew the reins out of his hands in the trot and canter.

The way the rider confronts the task will give the instructor a reason for discussing further strategy: Based upon her first attempt to "ride a circle," he clarifies new criteria with the rider. The functional relationship between the situation, the rider's movement, and the horse's movement must be explored by feel (i.e. experienced).

According to the horse's response, the instructor can draw a conclusion about the rider's movement and he can continue on this path of suggestions until the student is able to ride the movement appropriately and in accordance with the Riding Theory.

Developing the Rider's Ability to Recognize Function and Correlation

How the rider holds the reins, for instance, should not just be learned via verbal instruction that describes "how it should look," or be a simple attempt to imitate "how it should look." Instead, it must be developed from a deep understanding of the situation, the reins' function in that situation, and the mutual relationship between the rider's position and movement and the horse's position and movement—how they correlate. The rider must experience and explore through feel—

meaning consciously come to know—her position, its function, and the results of her movements as seen and felt in the horse's movement, through various exercises that help her understand how they interrelate. Cooperation and dialogue between riding instructor and rider enables the rider to gain insights from these experiences, which she can then apply to the next attempt of the same or similar exercise. This is how the rider is properly prepared to be able to ride independently and correctly, even without the riding instructor present.

Using Figurative Language

Research in the area of sports science shows that imagery helps the learning process—especially for beginners. Imagery outlines a generous framework for different ways of thinking about how to execute a movement. Here are some examples:

- Hold the reins as if you have a feather in your hand
- Sit as if you are light, almost weightless, like a winged fairy
- Imagine you are squeezing a sponge with your hands

Depending on the situation, the riding instructor has to think of shapes and images for the individual rider. By doing so, he accesses

Contrasting experiences in the saddle, such as leaning forward, stretching, and leaning down to the left and right, will enable the rider to find her individual correct seat.

the right side of the human brain, which is the location of visualization and processes information intuitively (without reasoning), randomly, and holistically.

Encourage Contrasting Experiences

Movements can be ridden slowly or fast, large or small, forcefully or lightly (see gymnastizing principles for the rider on p. 74). The rider must become sensitive to feeling and appreciating the differences in these variations of movement.

Whatever the correct form for the rider is at the moment—for instance, the correct seat—it can be found by performing contrasting exercises such as sitting to the extreme right, then to the extreme left, far forward or back. These contrasts serve to offer the brain a wide variety of possibilities and, by nature, the brain has the wisdom to find the best solution. After these exercises, it signals to the rider what the proper position is once she resumes her normal seat in the saddle. Striving for the correct seat while being given instruction often leads to a dead end. The rider tenses up because she is not allowed to search for the solution that feels best to her at the moment.

Seeing Movement Problems from the Rider's Perspective

In an *instruction-oriented* lesson, the instructor sees the riding problems from a perspective that cannot possibly be from the rider's perspective, otherwise the rider would change her riding position more quickly and with less difficulty. The fact that she cannot do this is because she cannot help it! Therefore, the instructor must approach her in a different way, by asking himself the following questions, for example:

What does the problem look like from the perspective of the rider? How does the rider feel now? What type of guidance (riding abilities and riding techniques) does she need in regard to horse and exercise? How precisely can he describe her riding problems, the horse's movement sequences, and the obstacles in the way of horse-and-rider interaction?

When the focus is on riding in conversation, instructions are not a sufficient solution for riding problems. The instructor must become receptive and be able to recognize the individual problems of horse and rider and not just be guided by an ideal formal visual appearance.

Instructors and Students Need to Communicate

It is still commonly accepted that the riding student in the "classroom" (during a lesson) should not speak but should only receive instruction. But, if the student does not speak, she has no way to communicate what she is experiencing in terms of the horse's and her movement sequences to her instructor. The student's experiences are important information for the instructor to consider when planning the next steps in a rider's education.

Specific rider behavior and the horse's resulting movement should be indications of the way a situation is being perceived by the rider. The instructor should build on this information, choose his strategy, and make it transparent to the rider.

Communication with the Rider

Another reference point for the instructor is the experience the rider gains from a movement. The instructor must conduct a dialogue with the rider in order to find out what the rider felt in a specific riding situation. The rider's behavior and her description of the way she felt the horse's movement will indicate how he can best proceed. Here, of course, it is necessary for the rider to become aware of her own perceptions and communicate them.

Directing the Rider's Attention

It is of fundamental importance to direct the student's attention and focus. The student's attention must be steered toward the particular elements, movement qualities, and other aspects of a specific situation that are most important to emphasize when seeking a certain outcome. By directing her attention, the instructor teaches the rider to actively analyze the riding lesson and in the process, experiment with different approaches that might result in a successful movement or exercise. The instructor should give the rider a task to execute, then ask her to feel how the horse changes when she uses different aids—softer versus harder ones, for example. The instructor can further highlight particular aspects of the movement as it is happening, calling the rider's attention to the results of her aids—and how they are being applied—so the rider knows to pay special attention to those details in the future. It is then the rider's job to filter out the relationship between what she feels (the horse's reactions) and how the function of her position and movement sequences influenced that result. There are virtually no limits to the observations the instructor can ask the rider to pay special attention to. He can use entire exercises: "Back your horse and afterward describe the horse's movement," or assign partial tasks: "Lighten your seat on the horse's back more, then less while asking him to back up, and describe the differences in the horse's movement."

Communication in Riding Instruction

In case of problems, the instructor must go to the student in order to start a dialogue to look for solutions together.

Conclusion: This *task-oriented* method has the goal of creating an independent rider who can conduct a conversation with the horse. The rider should be able to make decisions—for herself and for her horse—that are appropriate for any situation. The individual steps of a movement dictate the type of discussion between rider and horse. A lesson is not based upon strict instruction, instead, the rider is intensely involved in her own learning process right from the start.

Learning in this model also means learning in successive steps.

Task-Oriented Instruction—The Instructor's Approach

- Clarification of the movement's problem—the riding task.
- Clarification of the success criteria (application of aids).
- Execution of riding movements; analysis of the sequences; the next step is based upon this analysis.
- Creation of riding situations with progressive difficulty depending on the qualities of the horse and student.
- Providing individual solutions according to the rider's movement.
- During the following steps—depending on the type of developed movement solutions—the rider is encouraged to become aware of her own perceptions and to "listen" to the horse.
- Becoming aware of the rider's "internal" image (the rider's awareness of her body's movement) and asking the student about her movement solutions, her feel, and providing advice and solutions to moderate her riding movements.
- Finally, familiar (learned) riding lessons are applied, expanded, and analyzed together.

The Training Scale: The Familiarization Phase

The Significance of Familiarization

The "familiarization phase" is a technical term that incorporates the first three abilities of the horse's Training Scale, Rhythm, Suppleness, and Contact. All three are explained in more detail in the following pages. For the education of a young horse, this is the early schooling phase when the horse is made familiar with the fundamentals of riding. He should be taught to carry the rider's weight without losing his balance and also must learn the essential body-language signals of the rider: the aids. Most of all, however, during this familiarization phase the horse should be able to move just as naturally and freely under the additional weight of the rider as if he was not carrying a rider at all.

The term familiarization phase, however, does not only pertain to the basic training of a young horse, but to every warm-up phase: the goal of having the horse initially get used to the rider's weight, go in rhythm, be supple, and look for contact with the rider's hand equally applies to the beginning of every riding figure.

The significance of the three abilities Rhythm, Suppleness and Contact will be explained on the following pages. In addition, links between classical riding theory and biomechanics are meant to provide numerous tips for making this part of the riding education successful.

Contact is one of the three areas of ability of the Training Scale that are developed during the familiarization phase

Rhythm in the Young Horse

The first time the young horse starts moving under the rider is the difficult time in his development: he is "loaded" with the rider's weight. In principle, horses are able to carry weight, but only when the functionality of the musculature—especially the back and corresponding abdominal muscles—are developed for this purpose. The unfamiliar load on the horse's back (comparison: backpack on your back) can initially lead to upsets in rhythm. This disturbs—to various degrees—the naturalness of the horse's gait and thus the way movement is transferred to the rider.

Initially, the horse's back musculature arches toward the rider. Since the musculature is not yet fully developed, however, it will fatigue quickly, leading to slackening or sagging of the muscle groups.

The first goal during the early schooling phase is to reestablish the natural rhythm of the horse in each basic gait.

As a result, the back will start to sway, and the hindquarters become parked out. When the horse is now asked to move in the walk, trot, or canter, the sway back will have a negative effect on the gaits. What was a trot with a clean rhythm without the rider's weight will now become a gait with an uneven rhythm (no fluid movement from the back to front and vice versa).

Based on these facts, the rider is clearly required, first of all, to have a regulating influence on the horse's rhythm. This means, in detail, that the horse is brought back to his original situation (moving in rhythm without rider weight), but now with the rider's weight.

Regulating the Horse's Rhythm

Only a rider who has already developed proprioception is able to have a positive influence on the rhythm of the horse's gait, that is, to help the horse recover his rhythm under the rider.

In the opposite situation—an untrained rider on a schooled horse—the beginning of the familiarization phase means: Each riding

Rhythm in the Young Horse

situation must begin by having rider and horse find and align their natural rhythm during the movement, to have them find a common rhythm.

Conclusion: The first objectives of the basic training of the horse and at the beginning of each riding exercise is for the horse to find his rhythm and for the rider to adjust to this rhythm, or, create rhythm by skillfully influencing the horse in each gait (see practical tips in the individual gaits on p. 130).

Rhythm in the Three Basic Gaits

In each of the three basic gaits, the horse has a different rhythm, a different sequence of footfalls, and a different number of phases.

For a rider, who wants to acquire the feel for half-halts during her riding career, knowing about phases is important, but it is even more essential to feel what happens under the rider.

Many are able to "recite" the phases by heart, but they are unable to feel them and to draw respective conclusions for their application of aids. The rider must learn how to feel which one of the horse's legs is

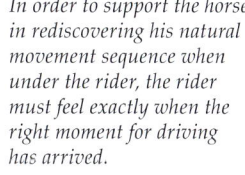

In order to support the horse in rediscovering his natural movement sequence when under the rider, the rider must feel exactly when the right moment for driving has arrived.

pushing off, when it is in the suspension phase, and when it touches the ground again, in order to find the right moment to apply her aids.

If the rider does not register the right moment, her influence—especially her driving aid—will be without effect. For example, when the rider doesn't drive at the moment when the horse flexes in the joints and is just about to push off, but instead drives at the moment of suspension. At this time, it is anatomically impossible for the horse to react to the rider's aids.

Rhythm at the Walk

The walk is a four-beat gait consisting of eight phases. It is the only gait without impulsion. This means that the walk does not have a

Take a deep breath: During a riding lesson, rider and horse should repeatedly incorporate active recovery phases. The reins are completely dropped, rider and horse can enjoy a brief time of relaxation.

The sequence of footfalls at the walk: There are always two or three feet on the ground. There is no suspension phase. Therefore the walk is considered without impulsion.

phase during which all four of the horse's legs are in suspension, there are always at least two feet on the ground. In principle, the walk is well-suited for teaching movement sequences. This slowest of the three gaits is the easiest in which to comprehend and practice new movement sequences for rider and horse. For this reason, the walk—within the framework of rider and horse education—is called the gait with "educational" character.

The walk is also important for the production of synovial fluid before the warm-up (see The Warm-Up on p. 63). Many aspects that were discussed in that chapter—respiration, heart rate, loosening of muscles, and so on—will not be discussed again at this point.

The walk is also used to incorporate active recovery phases during a riding lesson in order to allow the horse to regenerate.

Feeling Rhythm

There are a number of exercises to help riders develop a feel for the rhythm of the horse.

Bending Forward

Eyes closed, bend forward to the horse's neck, and touch the left and right sides of the horse's chest. You should say out loud when the left or the right front leg moves forward.

Bending over forward on the longe line at a walk is very helpful when teaching beginning riders a feel for the horse's movement sequence.

Bending Forward and Feeling the Sequence of Footfalls

Remaining in the same position, you should say when the left or right hind foot pushes off. If you have problems, your instructor can help you and announce when the horse's left or right hind foot pushes off. This aid will help you to feel the horse's movement more consciously and after that, you will most likely be able to identify them more quickly on the basis of feel.

Feeling the Sequence of Footfalls at the Walk

Ride in walk and follow the horse's footfalls (also with closed eyes). First, announce the movement of the front legs, then those of the hind legs. Afterward, you should also try to feel the sequence of footfalls as they relate to one another. For this purpose, you will assign each leg a number. The left front leg, for example, will be 1, the right hind leg 2, the right front leg 3, and the left hind leg 4.

Practical Notes

Drive Alternately at the Walk: The horse steps forward with alternate hind legs, which creates a palpable pendulum movement in the horse's rib cage. The pendulum-movement sequence requires the rider to drive *alternately*. The intensity of the driving aid depends on the extent to which the walk criteria (rhythm, eagerness, freedom of movement, length of stride) are fulfilled.

Allow the "Nodding" Movement of the Horse's Head: At the walk, the horse's neck is of special significance in its function as a balancing rod, since in this gait without impulsion, the forward movement is supported by a nodding movement of the neck. Therefore, it is essential that you allow this nodding movement. Otherwise, the horse's movement is unable to flow through his entire body. You must be able to follow the movement of the horse's head with your hands while continuously maintaining a soft, elastic connection from the hands to the horse's mouth. Therefore, when riding the walk, it is your hands that move the most.

Rhythm in the Trot

The trot is a two-beat gait with four phases, meaning a gait with

---

The Neck as a Balancing Rod

Especially at the walk, the horse must have the opportunity to maintain his balance by making nodding movements with his neck and head. When the rider shortens the reins too much, the horse will immediately lose his balance. The result: He is no longer in rhythm.

Rhythm in the Young Horse

impulsion and a suspension phase. The trot is most suitable for basic work. The rhythmic contraction and relaxation of all muscle groups makes it comparatively easy for the rider to adjust to the rhythm of the horse or to even stabilize the rhythm by skillful application of aids. For many horses, the trot is the best gait for suppling work.

Feeling the Sequence of Footfalls at the Trot: At the trot, say out loud when the left/right front leg and left/right hind leg push off and land on the ground.

Practical Notes

Driving Correctly: In principle, as described on page 52, driving should encourage the hind leg to step forward, thus creating an even flow of movement throughout the body. In the trot—a gait with impulsion—do not activate the hind leg on the same side; instead, always drive equally on both sides. Only later can the intensity of aids on the inside and outside be different.

During the rising trot, the rider alternately sits down and rises. Therefore, only every other trot step is supported by a driving aid.

The sequence of footfalls in the trot: One diagonal pair of the horse's legs lands at the same time, then pushes off into a suspension phase, then the other diagonal leg pair lands and again, pushes off into a suspension phase.

Sitting and Rising Trot: No matter whether you sit the trot or rise, the basic structure of driving is the same. During the rising trot, both of your lower legs move away from the horse while you are standing up. When sitting down, your legs touch the horse's body: both legs give the aid at the same time and influence the same side. During the rising trot, every second trot stride is supported by means of a driving aid; when sitting the trot, the driving aid can occur with every step—when needed. Just as in the walk, the intensity and frequency of the driving aid depends on the individual situation.

Rhythm in the Canter

Only when the horse moves forward securely and rhythmically under you in the trot can you add the canter work—at least in most cases. But the exception proves the rule: From time to time there are horses that have difficulty in becoming supple in the trot and feel much better when you give them the chance to first become supple in the canter—and only then in the trot. It is important for you to find out which gait the horse prefers.

The canter is a three-beat gait with six phases and—compared to the trot—a distinct suspension phase. In this gait, you must consider that the horse can be ridden on the right or on the left lead.

Feeling the sequence of footfalls in the canter: As in walk and trot, in the canter, say out loud when the inside/outside hind foot lands. There is no limit to the variation of these exercises.

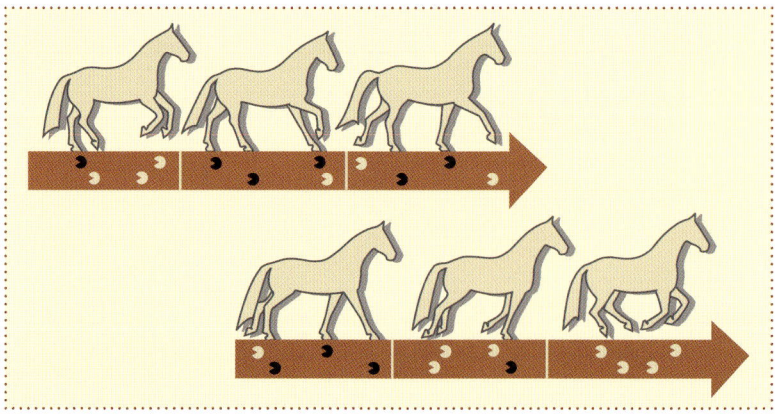

The sequence of footfalls in the canter on the right lead: The horse lands with the left hind leg, followed by the right hind leg and the left front leg at the same time. Then the right front leg lands, while the three remaining legs are in the air. Finally comes the moment of free suspension before the left hind leg lands once again.

The goal is for you to become aware of the horse's movement: to feel what goes on in the horse. This can help you conclude when to apply the various aids. Only when you clearly perceive the horse's movements, will you be able to consciously influence these movements.

Practical Notes

Strike Off at the Canter: Your guarding outside leg secures the horse's outside hind leg (supporting leg of the canter), which begins the canter. Using the half-halt technique, the horse is alerted to the coming new situation. Give the horse the necessary flexion, and guide his inside shoulder in front of the inside hip. This secures the positional requirements so that the horse "jumps" into the canter after shifting the weight to the inside seat bone in combination with the driving aid of the inside leg. The aids for striking off at the canter were already discussed on page 48.

The Rider's Three-Dimensionality

The Rider's "Engine": the Pelvis

The rider can feel the horse's swinging back if she is flexible in her pelvis and her movements are three-dimensional due to freedom in her sacroiliac joint. This three-dimensional flexibility of the rider's pelvis is essential for riding in each gait.

A "blocked" pelvis system is not only a problem for riders, but for all people. It is critical that several muscles are elastic: the deep back musculature, the gluteal muscles, the anterior and posterior thigh muscles, the iliopsoas, the abdominals, and the lateral musculature of the trunk.

The gluteal muscles must stabilize the pelvis; its function is often undone by an excessively shortened deep-back musculature. When this happens, there is a tendency to tilt the pelvis forward (the rider has a hollow back). This tendency is intensified by iliopsoas muscles that are too strong, which also position the pelvis into a hollow-back posture. If, additionally, the posterior thigh muscles are very strong, the rider cannot get out of this negative position, especially since the abdominals and gluteal muscles are often weak and cannot counteract

> **Flexibility of the Pelvis**
> Six muscle groups are responsible for the flexibility of the rider's pelvis. It is only possible to naturally swing with the movement of the horse's back when these six muscle groups are in harmony with one another.

the hollow back. It becomes impossible to naturally swing with the movement in the central neutral position (see p. 39).

The Pelvis Must Swing with the Movement
- The rider's deep, straight abdominal muscles must be strong enough to tilt the pelvis up (strengthening).
- The psoas muscles make the pelvis tilt forward; they are often too short (stretching).
- The obliques enable the one-sided weight aid without the shoulder having to move back (strengthening).
- The deep back musculature must not block movement (stretching).
- The gluteal musculature must also stabilize the pelvis and counteract the adductors at the same time. The gluteal muscles open the legs, the adductors close them (gluteals strengthening).
- The lateral musculature of the trunk is often not equally developed. It must be strengthened in order to be able to have a stabilizing effect (strengthening).

The twelve major problem areas of the rider: Weakened or shortened muscle groups stand in the way of supple riding. These weaknesses can be improved with the 6-Point Program (p. 35).

- The adductors can block the pelvis so they must be balanced in relation to the gluteal muscles. Most of the time, they are stronger than the gluteal muscles (adductors stretching).

The Sacroiliac Joint Must Be Free

Even when the described musculature is balanced and functioning harmoniously, you cannot swing with the horse's movement when your sacroiliac joint (SI joint) is blocked.

Many times, the cause of back problems arises in this joint area. The SI joint is an important joint for human beings since it can hinder the "naturalness" of movement sequences. All human movement is three-dimensional (forward/back, left/right, up/down).

Exercise for the Mobilization and Unblocking of the SI Joint

Start position: Lie on your back, one leg stretched, the other bent at a right angle in the hip and knee joint.
Exercise: Guide the angled leg across the stretched leg in the direction of the floor, whereby your hand can support the stretch. Turn your head in the opposite direction of the angled leg. Perform the exercise on both sides.

Almost every rider occasionally suffers from a block in the sacroiliac joint. With this simple exercise, the SI joint can be unblocked without a problem.

Suppleness

In rider terminology, Suppleness, the second ability on the Training Scale, is the relaxed contraction and relaxation of all flexors and extensors in the entire body of the horse. In their entirety, these are called the "muscle chain."

In connection with suppleness, we also often speak of "freedom from constraint." Freedom from constraint is the physical and mental state of relaxation that the horse should have naturally. It is also a precondition for the horse to later be able to develop suppleness under the rider. In contrast to freedom from constraint, suppleness is understood to be the relaxed flexing of muscles—or the alternate—flexing and relaxing.

A supple horse has regained the natural quality of his movement while under the rider's weight. A prerequisite for this is the horse going in rhythm (see p. 125).

Numerous indicators (ears, eyes, nostrils/mouth, throatlatch, neck, back, tail) will let the rider recognize or feel whether the horse is supple.

Causes of Inner "Tightness"

Many aspects of horse management can impact how more or less difficult it is to attain inner and outer suppleness in the horse. Typical sources of an inner "tightness" or lack of mental relaxation include: restlessness and boredom in the stall; too little roughage; stress; lack of exercise or too little turnout; and incorrect, inappropriate, or ill-fitting equipment.

In the general riding literature, there are two areas in regard to suppleness: *internal* and *external* suppleness (see the Rider's Training Scale on p. 71).

The respective explanations in the riding literature, however, are often insufficient since the reader tries to assign various body signs to the individual types of suppleness.

Suppleness must always be evaluated by looking at the overall "picture" of the horse and not by looking at his various individual body "signals" since these, in isolation, can distort the picture. *Internal* and *external* indicators of suppleness should, therefore, not be viewed in isolation, but always in correlation with each other.

Furthermore, the term "suppleness" does not only pertain to muscular work the horse performs, but to the horse's entirety as well: Psychological and physiological aspects play an equally important role.

We as riders must learn to understand the horse's body-language signals and explore what these signs mean. In order to provide a better understanding, we'll explain the characteristics separately below, in order to later combine them into an overall picture.

Indicators of Suppleness
The Head Area

Facial expression, ears, eyes, and nostrils display the countenance of the horse. The horse's behavior toward his handler should be natural and trusting, and he should perceive his environment in a relaxed state of mind with his ears focusing on surroundings.

This horse's facial expression shows that he is supple.

The horse's mouth area is of special significance. In the horse world, there is much mention of the closed, contentedly chewing and foaming mouth. Chewing is of particular relevance to the horse. Chewing—in its original meaning—always involves the intake of food first and then causes salivation. This is a reflex reaction: The chewing activity squeezes the sponge-like tissue of the parotid gland. Chewing therefore always produces saliva, whether a horse is supple or not; you can see this in an especially stressed horse—on the racetrack, for instance—that shows a considerable amount of saliva after running to the finish. This tells us that chewing serves as stress relief: The horse attempts to calm himself through chewing.

In a riding situation, the rider should prompt the horse to chew by influencing his mouth (see half-halts, p. 94).

The rider should understand that the musculature that triggers chewing is part of a muscle chain. She drives the horse from the back to the front and absorbs the movement energy with her subtle rein aids. In doing so, she moves the bit in the horse's mouth. This, in turn, influences the horse's muscle flexion, his chewing musculature is triggered, and this chewing causes salivation. This insight is not new. In the book *The Rider Forms the Horse* by Udo Bürger and Otto Zietzschmann, the authors clearly state that the chewing activity and frothing in the horse's mouth is only an attribute of quality when the horse keeps his lips closed while chewing!

Praise can contribute significantly to the development of a trusting relationship between rider and horse.

The Neck

One important indicator for suppleness is the horse's willingness to let his neck drop. In order to check whether the horse is willing to do so, the rider uses the exercise "giving the reins" in the trot. When the rider

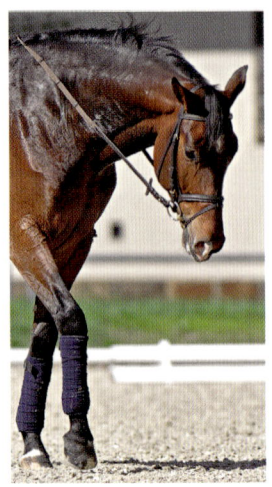

When "giving the reins," the head/neck angle opens up, and the poll is no longer at the highest point. Only in exceptional cases, however, should the horse lower his head as low as shown in the images below. As a rule of thumb, the horse's mouth should be at about the same level as the point of shoulder.

lets the rein slowly get longer while continuing to apply driving aids, the horse follows the rider's offer, while maintaining rhythm and pace, and stretches the neck with relaxed lower-neck musculature forward and down. In the process, the neck/head angle must open up otherwise the horse would no longer reach for the bit in this exercise. Depending on the horse's anatomical makeup, there is a rule of thumb for the dropped neck: The mouth can be lowered to about the level of the point of shoulder.

Respiration

When all of the horse's muscle chains are actively involved in the movement flow, this automatically leads to steady respiration, which can be expressed in snorting.

The Back

One of the most important criteria of suppleness is the horse's swinging back, which is also called the "center of movement." But an observer cannot reliably tell if the horse's back is swinging or tight without clues provided by the tail, head, and neck posture.

The most reliable indicator for a swinging back can be discerned by the rider and her feel. By means of the rhythmic contraction and relax-

ation of his muscles, the horse accepts the rider's weight and, therefore, allows the rider to "be able to sit and drive."

Suppleness needs to be within the rider as well as the horse so that the horse's back can swing. On the one hand, the horse's unconstrained contracting and relaxing musculature allows the rider to be able to sit and drive. On the other hand, the rider must be able to absorb the horse's movement and let it "flow" through her body three-dimensionally so that the horse gets supple in the back and starts swinging. Nowhere is the reciprocity between rider and horse more clearly illustrated than in the swinging back.

The Tail

The tail—as the extension of the back—is always viewed as the "seismograph" of the horse's muscle tone. If the back—as the horse's center of movement—contracts and relaxes rhythmically, working without constraint, this will be displayed in the tail carriage whether carried steadily, in unison with the movement rhythm, and swinging from left to right.

Practical Notes

There is no "one fits all" remedy that would be applicable for all horses in order to quickly make them supple during a riding session. For this particular ability, especially, it is the rider's *feel* that is critical: What the horse's condition is today, which exercises, and how many, will lead to meeting the goal for that particular day or riding session.

In general, however, we can say that frequent transitions from one gait to another can facilitate suppleness because the horse contracts and relaxes his musculature in different rhythms in each gait. For the majority of horses frequent transitions from one gait with impulsion to another, meaning from trot to canter and vice versa, are very effective. Also leg-yielding at the walk and the trot helps many horses to achieve suppleness, as do frequent changes of rein. In order to check for suppleness, the rider should integrate the exercise "giving the reins" into the end of the suppling phase.

A tail that swings in the rhythm of the movement is an important indication of suppleness.

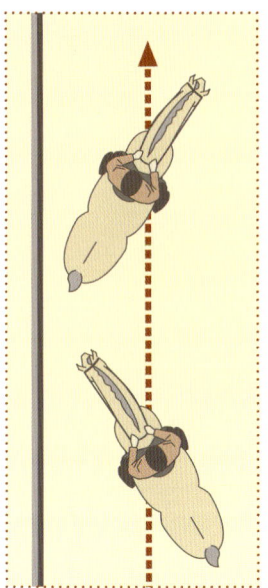
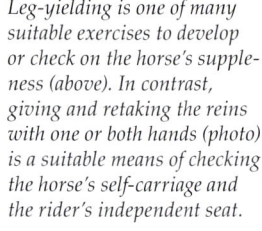

Leg-yielding is one of many suitable exercises to develop or check on the horse's suppleness (above). In contrast, giving and retaking the reins with one or both hands (photo) is a suitable means of checking the horse's self-carriage and the rider's independent seat.

Contact

The interplay of back activity and the horse's willingness to stretch provide the basis for the next point of the Training Scale: Contact. It is often mistakenly brought into play at the very beginning of a riding session or in the schooling of a young horse where the rider interferes with the rhythm of the horse's movement. In this context, you must differentiate between two aspects of contact: First, a very simple connection with the horse's mouth, which does, of course, exist from the start; second, contact in the sense of the Training Scale, when the horse "reaches for the bit."

The quality of Contact as it is referred to in the Training Scale can only occur after suppleness has been achieved, meaning the horse will trustingly reach for the bit.

These are the horse's preconditions for developing Contact:
- The horse moves in rhythm in all three basic gaits.
- There is a certain level of suppleness.

We only speak of correct contact when the horse accepts the rider's driving aid and steps toward the bit from back to front. In riding terminology we would then say: "The horse looks for contact and the rider allows it."

The interplay between the rider's driving and retaining aids are of critical importance for achieving contact. The horse first reacts to the driving impulse; then the effect of the connection between rider's hand and horse's mouth can be felt. Contact, therefore, does not merely pertain to rein influence; instead, it is the result of the rider's correct influence on the entire horse.

The rider's hand should allow constant contact while staying soft and elastic. As we've already noted, it is mandatory for the rider's hand to allow the nodding movements of the horse's head, which is most pronounced in the walk (see p. 130).

This alone makes it inevitable that constant contact to the horse's mouth should not be rigid, but must follow the movement of a constantly moving "system." Often, however, constant contact to the horse's mouth is mistakenly interpreted as "rigid holding of the rider's hand" with the rider trying to create a connection with the horse's mouth by merely shortening the reins.

A high-quality connection between rider's hand and horse's mouth must be possible at any time, no matter the neck posture of the horse. Therefore, it is irrelevant whether the horse has his poll as the highest point, or whether he "chews the reins out of the hand" opening the

Differences of contact (left hand giving the rein, right hand taking up the rein again) should not lead to the horse speeding up or slowing down. Comparing these two images, you can see that the horse's movement sequence is almost identical on a long rein and with a shorter rein, which is ideal.

After the related aids and with high-quality contact, the rider should be able to let the horse's neck drop and open the neck/head angle at any time.

neck/head angle. It must be possible for the horse to drop his neck at any time without losing the quality of contact.

Conclusion: A high-quality, steady contact cannot be achieved exclusively by attaining the two abilities of the Training Scale: Rhythm and Suppleness. Only by working on straightness and, therefore, on "pushing power," will a steady contact be improved. This again highlights the interplay between the six abilities. The best quality of contact (lightness) can only be achieved through development of Collection.

Creating Positive Tension

For the young horse, the end of the familiarization phase means he is now able to balance himself in all three basic gaits within his natural range of motion with a rider on his back, and he moves without constraint in all three gaits in rhythm and is willing to reach for the bit.

In practical application within a riding session, the end of the familiarization phase means that horse and rider are warmed up and

The rider can improve the horse's straightness by means of half-pirouettes in walk (left). In order to check Rhythm, Suppleness, and Contact at the walk, the rider gives the rein.

prepared for further training, i.e. all muscle chains are now "working."

During the entire familiarization phase, the rider must concentrate on the task of leading the horse back to his natural movement in spite of the additional weight of the rider. This is basis for subsequent schooling work: No changes have yet been made to the horse's paces, but this will be developed for the first time when you start to focus on Impulsion, the next ability of the Training Scale (see p. 148).

At a Glance

- The term "familiarization phase" encompasses the first three areas of ability in the Training Scale: Rhythm, Suppleness, and Contact.

- The first objective when schooling the young horse is to reestablish his natural rhythm under the rider's weight.

- The rider must be able to correctly drive the horse in the rhythm of the basic gaits and be able to follow the horse's swinging back movements with her pelvis.

- Suppleness is defined as "unconstrained contraction and relaxation of all the skeletal muscles—flexors and extensors—in the horse's body." Indications of the horse's suppleness are very multi-faceted, and every rider should know them (p. 137).

- The quality of the third ability, Contact, can only be developed after achieving Suppleness. Contact is defined as the horse's ability to trustingly—and bilaterally—step toward the rider's hand.

- During the familiarization phase, the rider creates the prerequisites for subsequent schooling work. When these preconditions do not exist, subsequent schooling will be riddled with problems.

Impulsion, Straightening, and Collection

From Familiarization to Pushing and Carrying Power

During the familiarization phase, the young horse is schooled to stretch toward the rider's hand, in rhythm, and with rhythmically contracting and relaxing musculature.

The familiarization phase—teaching Rhythm, Suppleness, and Contact—is viewed as the warm-up phase of a riding session for the more advanced horse. It is necessary to prepare the horse with these abilities. In doing so, the horse develops the necessary positive tension, which is a precondition for the upcoming work. The development of *pushing power* marks the beginning of the advanced schooling of the horse.

All abilities that have been developed in the young horse so far serve the purpose of restoring the horse to his natural state when under the rider.

All subsequent schooling work has the objective of making the horse more athletic and continuing to develop him according to his natural predisposition and talent.

From the athletic perspective, the most important aspect is to beautify and expand the horse's movement and to enable him to move under the rider with increased athleticism, harmony, and lightness.

It is not just for use in sports that it is necessary to develop the three advanced areas of ability in the horse: Impulsion, Straightening, and Collection. Only the rider who sufficiently schools her horse in all six abilities of the Training Scale can be sure that her horse will remain healthy for riding, whether for competition or recreation, and bring joy and trust that risks will be kept to a minimum.

Advanced Development of the Horse

During the course of advanced development, all abilities are perfected interdependently; that is, all abilities are mutually dependent on one another. For this purpose, the horse must continue to develop on two levels: *coordination* and *condition*.

On page 17, we discussed the *coordinative* abilities of the rider. Now, we will summarize them briefly as they pertain to the horse. The goal is for the horse to stabilize his Balance and Rhythm while incorporating Impulsion, Straightening, and Collection. The more the horse's schooling progresses, the higher the demands that are placed on the horse's coordination and condition.

In dressage, lessons like piaffe and passage require the most from the horse and rider; in jumping, it is the high jumps and difficult distances between obstacles; in eventing, it is about increasingly complex technical tasks. The main requirements, however, continue to be the initial abilities: Rhythm and Suppleness, which must be maintained in every movement. When this doesn't happen, the reason is usually to be found in the horse's balance. A deficit in Rhythm and Suppleness has a negative effect on all other abilities—among other things: responsiveness; visual orientation; ability to use muscles in different ways depending on the footing of the riding arena; the flow of movement through the entire body from the hindquarters to the mouth and back; and coordination of impulses. The ultimate goal is for the horse's movement to be lighter, more elegant, and harmonious, all of which can be achieved by increasing his coordination.

The horse will develop his *condition* in the areas of *speed, strength* and *endurance* during this stage of schooling: He increasingly becomes an athlete. *Speed* means the ability to perform required movements within the shortest possible time. The horse pushes off faster and more dynamically and is able to land on the ground smoothly and, after the foot lands on the ground, performs subsequent movement with such softness that it is fluid, not choppy.

For this purpose, the horse requires *strength* (when the foot pushes off and lands) since strength always corresponds with speed. It is essential that increased muscle development is coupled with flexibility and dynamic ability. Development of strength must always occur in the context of the physical structure (an individual horse's body type and his intended purpose), because an excess of strength can have a negative effect on the horse's mobility and flexibility.

Endurance means that the horse can perform a movement (e.g. a half-pass or a long canter stretch) not only once, twice, or three times, but can "recall" this movement at even higher repetition rates. His ability to absorb oxygen is increased and his pulse rate is lowered since the heart is able to pump more blood with one beat. In this

Advanced Development
Advanced development of the horse according to the Training Scale is only possible when the areas of ability in the familiarization phase, Rhythm, Suppleness, and Contact are mastered.

context, his ability to repeat a movement does not pertain to a monotonous number performed, but rather that the same movement can be reproduced in different ways, in different places, and to different extents. Endurance corresponds with the two other conditions of *speed* and *strength*, mentioned earlier.

The more challenging and complex the requirements of the lessons become for the horse, the more he develops his condition and coordination, both of which are needed for extending the trot or tight turns, for example.

Actively Changing Movement

By developing impulsion, the rider gains the horse's ability to change his frame and his ground cover in all the gaits. This is what the rider is striving for when developing impulsion. By using various transitions appropriately, the rider can school the horse to use his movement energy more consciously in order to perform larger steps or strides, for example. The main objective is a more powerful push-off and an expansion of the movement amplitude.

Impulsion

In rider terminology, "impulsion" (in German, *Schwung*) is divided into:
- Moving in a gait with impulsion.
- Working with impulsion.

The difference between moving in a gait with impulsion and working with impulsion is of enormous significance. Moving in a gait with impulsion is the horse's natural predisposition to move forward in trot and canter, in these gaits that have a suspension phase.

Nowadays, many horses are born with a lot of quality of movement. To say that these horses are "working with impulsion," however, is not always correct in the sense of the classical Riding Theory: Working with impulsion does not just pertain to a movement sequence; it means that the horse must perform it in a state of suppleness.

There are plenty of horses that show quality of movement when they are "under tension."

By means of a sophisticated interplay of driving and retaining aids and the correct application of half-halts, the rider wants a supple horse that pushes off energetically with the hindquarters, with the resulting impulse of energy being transferred throughout his swinging back into his entire forward movement.

For example, in the trot, the horse should step more under his body, and outline a longer "arc" with the hind and front legs. The horse will only be able to do this if he can lengthen the suspension. In riding terminology, this can be summarized as follows: The horse should be "a short time on the ground, and a long time in the air."

An energetic hindquarters push-off, however, is not the only indication of working with impulsion. It is equally visible in the way the horse lets the powerful impulse of energy "through" the back to the mouth then back to the hindquarters. The arc of the stride does not only change in the hindquarters, but also in the forehand. This means that when the rider works on developing the horse's impulsion, he changes the horse's ground coverage: The arc of the horse's footfall becomes wider, the front and hind legs swing forward more, and

---

Development of Impulsion

The goal of developing impulsion in all three basic gaits is for the horse to be able to expand his stride and the amount of ground covered by his footfalls and adjust his frame. For these purposes, he must push off more energetically and increase the "size" of his movement.

swing higher, the suspension phase becomes longer, and the push-off phase seems to get shorter, when in reality, however, it simply becomes more powerful.

Canter and trot are called gaits with impulsion because they have a suspension phase. The canter is the gait with the longest suspension phase.

Anatomical Background

Good impulsion in the sense of the Training Scale is developed from the horse's hind end and—in a supple horse—flows like a "springing" impulse from behind over the back to the mouth. This circle of energy is closed when the impulse travels from the mouth back to the rider's driving and retaining aids and once again arrives at the horse's hindquarters.

Lengthening the stride in trot: The large joints of the hindquarters—hips, stifles, and hocks—move forward with more range of motion.

Many people today only look at the forelimbs when evaluating a horse's impulsion. It is much more important, however, to check whether the hind feet reach beyond the tracks of the front feet and also observe the direction of movement of the horse's hocks. Their anatomical design is such that their movement direction provides insights into the question as to whether the horse is on the correct path toward the development of working with impulsion.

When developing impulsion, it is not only a matter of the direction of movement of the hocks, but also a matter of the so-called "large joints" of the horse: the hip, stifle, and hock joints. At this point in schooling, the goal is to ensure energy development from the hindquarters. This changes the magnitude of the horse's movements. First, the "large joints" move forward with greater scope. This development of the energy from the hindquarters is a central point for the continued schooling of the horse; you often hear of impulsion as being a sort of "door opener" for subsequent work on collection.

The first objective is to change the direction of movement of the large joints. The second objective is to improve the ability to flex the large joints (more about this topic on p. 179).

However, it is not the forward movement of the hip or stifle joints that can be seen well from the ground, but rather the hock joints, which, in response to the rider's driving aid, are supposed to move forward and upward, not merely pull up or swing out to the back. Nowadays, you can often see horses in top-class dressage competition that show extreme upward movement with the front legs but do not bring the hind legs under the body sufficiently. Instead, the horse swings them out to the back and, therefore, cannot transfer the energy impulse from behind through his back. The arc of the footfall of this horse also changes—too much upward and too little forward. As a result, the horse's ground cover is decreased instead of increased.

What Does the Rider Feel?

Whether the rider is on the right path to initiate the development of working with impulsion with his horse can be seen from the ground by an observer, but the rider can "feel" it. However, the rider, with her flexible pelvis, must be able follow the movement of the horse's back as it becomes more pronounced by the changed size and scope of the horse's stride. When the rider is able to adjust to the lengthening of the frame and to "let the horse move her," she can influence the impulsion of the horse. A good way to check this is to ride transitions within a gait, meaning a change of pace from working trot to medium trot, or back to the collected trot.

A successful canter extension on a curved line.

The Rider's Influence for Developing Impulsion

In order to achieve impulsion in the horse, the rider must create an energetic impulse from the horse's hindquarters by driving with more energy herself. In the process, the rider can only "be moved by the horse" when she drives correctly: not allowing herself to become blocked in the pelvis and keeping her upper body erect or slightly tilting forward from the pelvis. In this posture, the rider is able to allow the horse to lengthen his frame in the neck.

In order to correctly use her muscles for driving, the rider should slightly open out her leg, meaning that the tip of the foot points a little to the outside. If you imagine the face of a clock, the tip of your left foot is the 11, the tip of the right foot on the 1. When you hold the feet parallel to the horse's body (as riding instructors still often ask for), your calves can only be used for driving if the adductors are used, but this causes the pelvis to lock up and you can no longer be moved by the horse's movement. You would sit against the movement of the horse and hinder or even prevent the horse's impulsion.

By having the tips of the feet slightly pointing to the outside, you are able to utilize your calves as a driving impulse by flexing and relaxing the muscles on the back of the thigh (knee flexors). This musculature is very strong and can be applied in a flash. If the stirrups are too long, however, the muscles on the back of the thighs can't really be used, even if the tips of the feet slightly point outward. Instead, the gastrocnemius muscles below the knee take on this function (before the knee flexors can act) and they pull your heel up. This will cause the pelvis to tilt backward so that it can no longer properly follow the movements of the horse's hindquarters and back.

Rider Requirements

The rider is only able to develop movement with impulsion, when her pelvis is flexible to all sides. Her pelvis must function three-dimensionally (to the front and back, left and right, up and down; see The Rider's Three-Dimensionality p. 133). This three-dimensionality of the pelvis only exists if the sacroiliac joint is unencumbered so before mounting, the rider should always check the freedom of movement of the sacroiliac joint by performing a special exercise (p. 135), in order to be able to softly sit the horse's impulsion during the suspension phases (trot and canter) and be able to let the horse move her.

Overall, the rider must be as flexible as possible in the pelvis. Her pelvis movements to the right and left (on the face of a clock from 3 to 9) and to the front and back (from 6 to 12) should be of identical size in order to support the horse in the development of impulsion, instead of having a blocking effect. If there are indeed differences,

To develop impulsion in the horse, the rider must be able to differentiate and use the muscles in her body involved in the driving aids. Her goal is that with an amplified driving aid, she will increase the energy coming from the horse's hindquarters.

they can be adjusted by the pertinent exercises on the Balimo Chair (p. 46).

It should be the rider's goal to create a slight forward tendency of the upper body by tilting the pelvis, without sitting in front of the movement. (The weight aids must still be effective.) This posture also moves the hands slightly forward in order to support the entire movement flow of the horse by means of soft contact, and to allow a lengthening of the frame during extensions, also the neck area. In order to carry out such movements without any issues, the rider's pelvic movements must react at the horse's speed with utmost flexibility and softness so that she will not get behind the horse's movement in the first place. In addition, she must have control over her rein coordination to an extent that she is able to skillfully yield and shorten the reins with her hands—independently from the basic seat. To summarize, the following criteria are important as movement pertains to the rider:

- Freely movable SI joint.
- Flexibility of the pelvis in all directions.
- Stirrups under the widest part of the balls of the foot.
- Rider's gaze must be slightly below the horizontal.
- Stirrups must be correct length (no stretching down into long stirrups, which reduces the flexibility of the pelvis).

> **The Pelvis: Motivator or Blocker?**
>
> The rider's pelvis should flexibly and "three-dimensionally" follow the horse's back. Especially important for the development of impulsion is for the rider to let her pelvis follow reactively, according to the driving aids.

Impulsion and the Rider's Seat

As a result of the development of impulsion, the rider's upper body may fall back due to the horse's strong forward drive. This is undesirable since the upper body—when leaning back—automatically "fixes" the pelvis and in the process, blocks the junction between the fifth lumbar vertebra and the sacrum. This disturbs the horse's entire movement and causes rhythm or tension problems.

During transitions, the rider must balance her pelvis in a way that will not hollow her back and disturb the horse's back. By tilting backward with the upper body, she can also influence the reins incorrectly, thus disturbing the horse's mouth. The consequence could reduce the entire forward drive of the horse from the hind leg through his back to his mouth; flow of movement is impeded, and

While slowing down, here from an extended trot back to working trot, it is important to maintain sensitive contact with the reins. If the rider starts "pulling," she will "block" the horse's movement.

the *positive tension* function used by the horse to obtain "spring" is largely disabled.

In this way, it is impossible to achieve the objective of this schooling phase: the lengthening of the horse's frame and self-carriage.

Decreasing Impulsion

The rider needs to hold the reins with great sensitivity during a transition to slower impulsion; the hand must not have a blocking effect. The rider's driving aid must still cause the horse's hind legs to continue to swing or jump forward even when slowing down, in order to enable the horse to take "on load" fluidly. It is imperative to maintain the impulsion that was already developed while slowing down! From the perspective of the rider's seat and influence, she can only achieve this if she has excellent balance, understands the subtle connections between driving and retaining aids, and knows how to appropriately utilize them in changing situations—meaning, in this case, the half-halt technique.

The transition is achieved by "tucking in the belly button," which causes the pelvis to slightly tilt back and down, a movement that the horse interprets as putting more weight into the saddle (weight aid). "Tucking in the belly button" puts pressure on the rider's back, however, it doesn't block the back since the rider's pelvis maintains flexibility in spite of being under pressure. You can immediately feel when the horse accepts this aid and when doing so, he will not "fall" onto the bit, but rather maintain a fluid forward movement.

In rider terminology, a different phrase has been established to describe the tucked-in belly button: "bracing the back." But, anatomically, it is completely impossible to brace the back. In addition, many riders associate a completely different process with the phrase "bracing the back": They tilt their upper body behind the vertical, fix their pelvis by tightly contracting their abdominal and gluteal muscles, and, consequently, block the horse's back.

In order to prevent misunderstandings, saying "bracing the back" should be replaced by "tucking in the belly button," where the pelvis slightly tilts backward, shifts more weight onto both seat bones, but stays flexible and does not block the horse in the back. While doing so, the rider exhales. It is important that the rider understands what actually happens when slowing down impulsion from the anatomical and physiological perspective. During the process of slowing down impulsion, the "character" of a half-halt is perfectly implemented. This represents one of the greatest challenges to the rider.

> **"Tucking in the Belly" instead of "Bracing the Back"**
>
> Slightly tilting the pelvis while slowing down impulsion is described as "bracing the back." It is more precise to describe this process as "tucking in the belly button." Anatomically, it is not possible to brace the back, anyhow.

Impulsion at the Walk?

It is paradoxical to speak of *impulsion* in the context of the walk. How can a horse show movement sequences with impulsion in a gait that doesn't have a suspension phase? This once again illustrates that the term impulsion needs to be explained more fully to riders. Impulsion is an energetic impulse from the horse's hindquarters, through his body, that affects his entire forward movement. The word "energy" can just as well be applied to the walk (a gait without impulsion) but because the word "impulsion" is easily misunderstood it would be better to say the horse eagerly moves forward at the walk, with energy from the hind end and through the body.

However, of all three basic gaits, it is most difficult for the rider, first of all, to trigger then "control" an energetic impulse at the walk. Therefore, it is the last gait to be schooled when it comes to the development of impulsion. This is reflected in dressage tests: Up to and including Second Level, the rider is only required to show at medium walk. But starting with Third Level, the walk shown in the tests

> **Impulsion—At the Walk**
>
> Even though the walk is a gait without impulsion and a suspension phase, it is actually possible to develop the ability of impulsion at the walk.

becomes more advanced: first by adding the collected walk, and later the extended walk.

As stated, the term "impulsion" means an energetically pushing-off hind leg with a changing arc of footfall. This is equally possible in gaits with impulsion as it is in the gait without impulsion—the walk. However, at the walk, it is equally possible to encourage the horse to step *farther forward* with the foot describing a *flat arc*, or to step forward *not as far* with the foot describing a rather *high arc*. Since the walk does not have a suspension phase, it makes a high demand on the rider's interplay of the driving and retaining aids. While there is—merely by the fact that there is a suspension phase—a predominately clear rhythm to be felt at the trot and canter, it is much harder for the rider to "feel for" the clear beat and rhythm at the walk. In regard to the beat, the walk is also considered the most "interference-prone" gait.

Tips for Riding the Walk

Since the walk movement is three-dimensional, freedom of movement in the rider's sacroiliac joint becomes even more important. Any small misalignment of the joint has a grave effect on the quality of the walk (four-beat, freedom of movement, eagerness, and ground coverage). Therefore, the rider should perform exercises to check the freedom of movement of the SI joint (pp. 39 and 135) and ensure that her pelvis is flexible in all directions. It is necessary to have optimal flexibility in all directions since any weakness of the pelvis will negatively influence the four walk criteria (see above).

In the process, the rider must not push with her pelvis since this movement disturbs the flexibility of the horse's back. The weight aids are passively supportive, you drive with the lower legs or calves. You must sit erect so that your weight can function as a supportive aid. Your "throughness" can be observed when you—just like the horse—show a "nodding" movement, which must not, however, exceed a certain extent. When your head and neck area is tense (see 6-Point Program on p. 35), it must be loosened by means of respective exercises. Otherwise, your flow of movement will not function and the horse's walk will (unintentionally) be disturbed.

The rider's hip flexors must also be elastic, so she can let her legs fall into the stirrups, relaxed, and as long as possible and as necessary.

However, it is also important to ensure that the stirrups are not too long, as they can often be seen today, because it can hinder the flexibility of the pelvis. The longer the stirrup, the more the rider hollows the back and a higher heel results. The shorter the stirrup, the higher the knee, the pelvis tilts to the back, and the rider sits with a round back. The leg must also not be stretched into the stirrup, since this also fixes the pelvis. At the walk, it is also especially important for the rider to step into the stirrup with the widest part of the ball of her foot. Only when in this posture can the rider let the movement "flow out to the bottom," meaning able to stay reactive and elastic in the ankle joints. This, of course, applies equally to trot and canter.

When the leg position fulfills these conditions, the rider can support the horse with her driving aids. At the walk, she drives alternately with both legs. When the horse has developed four-beats, freedom of movement, eagerness, and ground coverage, the entire leg now only "goes with" or "manages" the horse, meaning the rider's relaxed legs swing at the horse's body ("the horse picks up the leg aid," as is often said by riders.) Due to the leg's close contact with the horse the rider is able to softly influence the horse at any time, whenever the walk criteria are lost. Nowadays, unfortunately, we see time and again how riders clamp with their legs or drive every step out of the horse. Riders should refrain from doing so since the leg dictates the pace to the horse, which he then should maintain. Constant driving, however, (also in other gaits) makes horses lazy. The horse must respect the leg, not become dulled by it.

When the rider changes the length of the horse's steps, she also develops his ability to maintain balance. If the horse is able to change

In order to achieve the four criteria of a good walk (four-beat, freedom of movement, eagerness, and ground coverage), the rider's pelvis must be absolutely relaxed. Any misalignment or blockage can lead to a loss of quality in the walk.

At the walk, rein influence must be handled very carefully. This rider succeeds in doing so perfectly: She is allowing the horse's nodding movement, so he can open up his head and neck angle.

the length of his steps, he requires a more pronounced balance. This applies to the other gaits along the same lines, apart from the fact that there is an added suspension phase in trot and canter. By developing impulsion in every gait, the rider creates the possibility of actively improving the horse's balance.

How to Develop Eagerness (Impulsion) at the Walk

Transitions Within the Walk: First, eager forward movement; actively allow/support nodding movements with a soft, forward moving hand.

Collection: Repeatedly ride sets of a few shortened steps; aids in the process: continue to drive, the hand still going softly with the movement and giving careful retaining impulses (i. e. "tucking in the belly button," half-halts); ensure that the horse maintains the beat.

Suitable Exercise—Half-Pirouette at the Walk: The half-pirouette at the walk already has a "collecting" character. The focus at this point of schooling is, however, to develop eagerness at the walk. When riding into the turn, shorten the steps. From the shortened strides it is then easier for horse and rider—after the turn—to have the horse step toward the hand. This makes it easier to develop steps that have more ground coverage. Once collection is developed, pirouettes at the walk (turning on a smaller diameter) can help to solidify this principle: On the one hand, ground coverage is improved (extended walk), on the other, collection, also.

> **Improving the Walk by Driving More?**
> Due to the fact that it is a gait without impulsion, the walk is considered the most difficult and "interference-prone" gait. Many riders believe that they can improve this gait by simply driving more. This, however, will disturb the beat rather than improve it.

Development of Impulsion in the Trot

Walk/Trot Transitions: The focus must be on *forward movement* at the moment of an energetic push-off. While the horse promptly moves off into the trot, there should be a lot of energy flowing from the hindquarters through the body.

Canter/Trot Transitions: Initially, suppling trot/canter transitions, then canter/trot transitions. In order to change the movement's "size" in trot, transition from canter into trot. As soon as the horse finds the beat of the trot, immediately lengthen the steps for a few yards. Out of this forward movement of the trot, the horse will develop a lot of energy from the hindquarters. These canter/trot transitions, however, only help to achieve the objective when the horse is supple. If suppleness has not yet been established, this exercise would only prompt the horse to transition back into the canter, instead of lengthening the steps after transitioning into the trot.

Transitions Within the Trot: Frequent change between working trot and extended trot. When extending the steps, you must be sure the horse is really able to lengthen his frame, meaning you slightly tilt your pelvis forward and your hand moves forward as a result so that he is able to

Impulsion, Straightening, and Collection

Frequent transitions within the trot are suitable exercises to continue development of impulsion in this gait. The goal is to have the hindquarters actively step forward. As a guideline, look at the horse's forearm and hind cannon bone. Ideally, they are almost parallel to each other, which is not the case in this photo quite yet.

use his neck as a balancing rod to be able to perform the larger movement sequences in balance. When slowing down, your pelvis is taken back a bit more by your "tucking in the belly button," which causes increased pressure on the ischial tuberosity (seat bones). You can use these transitions to check and fine-tune the horse's half-halt technique. As soon as you are successful in having the horse not "lean" on your hand when slowing down, but having him shorten his steps and strides via half-halts in self-carriage, the horse has let your half-halts go "through."

Development of Impulsion in the Canter

Trot/Canter Transitions: Ensure that the horse energetically pushes off from the trot and jumps into the canter with a forward and upward direction. Think about speeding up when moving off into the canter; ride the first few canter strides more freely forward.

Transitions Within the Canter: When speeding up and slowing down in the canter, always be sure that the horse carries himself and does not lean on your hand (use half-halts). When slowing down, especially, horses at first have a hard time. Initially, it is helpful to combine slowing down with riding a curved line. For example: Speed up on the long side, then slow down at the middle of the long side by riding a large, curved line, such as a circle. While doing so, give and retake the reins in order to check whether the horse is carrying himself. From there, speed up again, and once again slow down at the end of the long side, in the corner. As the horse's schooling progresses, the curved lines can be decreased in size down to a volte.

When speeding up in the canter, the hindquarters should step farther under the horse's body. But this is not enough: The developed impulsion must flow through the horse's body and must not cause the horse to pull his head and neck too much out of the rider's hand.

Straightening

The Significance of Straightening

In the opinion of many riders, straightening—just like impulsion—has reached a certain point in the horse's schooling that mainly applies to dressage horses. But every horse—whether in dressage, jumping, or eventing, performance or recreational—should be straightened, for health reasons alone. Only a "straight" horse is able to withstand the demands of being under a rider without suffering adverse effects in the long term. A jumper must be straightened, once he has learned to collect, so he is able to powerfully push off with the hindquarters and land elastically without suffering wear and tear. A recreational horse

Straightening on a curved line: The rider has given her horse the exactly correct amount of flexion and bend in order to canter on the track of the circle. The horse's inside right hind leg is stepping under the body in a slight diagonal.

that is expected to be able in the long term to travel long stretches over country must be able to equally load all four legs. A horse that continuously moves crookedly under the rider will wear out his joints and ligaments quickly on one side, develop his musculature differently on the left and right, and not be able to compensate for the resulting tension over the long term.

When a trainer starts to work on straightening, the horse is usually in his second year of schooling. This is also reflected by dressage

tests: Up to First Level only requires that the horse is starting to straighten; a certain crookedness—for instance, when cantering along the long side—is still tolerated. By the time the horse enters Second Level, the horse must be straightened as a mandatory prerequisite for collection.

Collective Goal: Pushing Power

By incorporating straightening, it becomes possible to develop so-called "pushing power" in the horse. The abilities of the Training Scale, Impulsion and Straightening contribute to the development of pushing power. The common objectives of impulsion and straightening through suitable exercises (see p. 170), is for the horse to gain the ability not only to maintain his balance when riding straight ahead in the three basic gaits, but also balance himself when the demands on movement become more complex and sophisticated.

The demands started to increase with the work on impulsion where the goal was to change the horse's ground coverage. This created the prerequisites for straightening. During the course of his continued schooling in straightening, the horse should solidify his pushing power from the hindquarters.

Only by straightening the horse can you make both sides of the horse's body equally supple and able to move and load his joints equally on the right and left side. Furthermore, straightening is a precondition for flexing the horse's large joints. This, in turn, is the most important goal during subsequent work on Collection. Straightening, therefore, has two equally important objectives: keeping the horse sound by preventing unilateral wear and tear, and creating the necessary preconditions for collection.

What Does "Straightening a Horse" Mean?

In his natural state, the horse is never straight but has a so-called "natural crookedness." Simply said, this means that the horse moves differently when riding turns to the right as compared to the left. In about 80 percent of horses, the right hind leg tracks to the right going *past* the front leg on the same side. This happens when going straight ahead as well as during turns. In contrast, the left hind leg tracks toward the direction of the horse's center of gravity, to the right. You

> **Straightening Applies to all Horses!**
>
> In order to enable a horse to carry the load of the rider without suffering adverse health effects, the rider must ensure that his muscles, tendons, joints, and ligaments are equally stressed on both sides. This is achieved by Straightening, a method of maintaining the horse's health no matter his discipline. It is not a "dressage-focused" end in itself.

could say, "The right hind leg steps 'out of the load,'" and "The left hind leg steps 'into the load.'"

The rider, while riding straight ahead or during turns, feels more pressure on the left rein, while the right rein is often not accepted, (meaning there is no connection between the rider's hand and the horse's mouth). This crookedness of the horse is amplified by his anatomy, since the hips are wider than the shoulders.

The goal of straightening is to have the horse "track up." This can be explained as follows: When a horse moves straight ahead, it should be possible to draw two lines, onto which the horse would place his front and hind feet. These lines are called "tracks." To enable the horse to move on two tracks while riding straight ahead, the rider must align the (narrower) forehand to the (wider) hindquarters by bringing the inside shoulder in front of the inside hip. The horse's forehand is slightly "offset" to the inside in front of the hindquarters. To make sure that the horse actually only moves on two tracks, he must not only evenly track forward with his hindquarters, but also move slightly diagonally to the inside in the direction of the tracks of the front hooves.

> **Anatomical Challenge**
> Due to the anatomical structure of the horse (his forehand is narrower than his hind end), straightness can only be achieved when the hindquarters are at a slight angle to the forehand.

What Does the Rider Feel?

When riding straight ahead on a horse that is not yet straightened, the rider often feels that the horse steps toward the left rein, and that it is impossible to create a connection on the right rein. As described above, most horses step "out of the load" on the right hind side meaning past the front leg on the right, and "into the load," meaning more under the center of gravity, on the left side.

During turns to the *right*, the right hind leg also tracks "out of the load," meaning, in this case, toward the inside. Since the rider cannot create a connection to the horse's mouth on the right side, she initially does not succeed in bringing the inside shoulder in front of the inside hip.

When riding turns toward the *left*, however, the rider has the feeling that the horse tenses up and gets stiff. He does not step toward the right outside rein and, instead, "leans" on the left inside rein. The neck muscle remains stiff; the crest stays on the right side instead of tilting to the left. The horse seems to stay bent to the right, even during turns

Straightening

A straightened horse in the canter: You can clearly see from the front as well as the back that the forehand has been brought slightly toward the inside in front of the inside hip.

to the left. The hindquarters do not follow the track of the forehand, but instead drift out of the turn.

From the feeling that the rider has on a naturally crooked horse, arose the various terms for describing the right and left half of the horse's body. The *left side*, that feels tighter to the rider, is called "stiff side," and the *right side* is called the "hollow side" since the horse seems to make himself hollow on this side without, however, accepting as much load as desired with his hindquarters.

The Rider is Shifted

For the rider, this feeling can be unpleasant at first. The experienced rider feels that she cannot sit "in the center" of the horse and can no longer evenly load her ischial tuberosities (seat bones). It seems to her

A correct leg-yield requires straightness of horse and rider achieved through gradual lessons over time.

the horse has shifted her. The anatomical and physiological explanation: Since the right hind leg does not step under the center of balance of the horse, the right side of the horse's rib cage bulges up more than the left—no matter whether you ride straight ahead, to the right or to the left. Due to this slight bulge of the rib cage, it is not possible for the rider to sit straight in the saddle and evenly load both seat bones.

The result: The center of gravity of the rider's body changes; she is shifted to the left (an inexperienced rider often compensates by collapsing in the right hip).

What Happens When the Horse is Straightened?

The objective of straightening is that the rider must try in every gait and while riding straight ahead and during right and left turns, to bring the inside (narrower) shoulder in front of the inside (wider) hip (see drawing on p. 90). This, in turn, means that the horse must basically be permanently slightly flexed and bent (see "riding in flexion" on p. 167). Only then can the rider bring the respective inside shoulder in front of the inside hip.

Interestingly, the specialized literature usually only describes this technique for the canter. For example, a horse cantering on the right lead should be slightly flexed and bent to the right, and the right shoulder should be brought in front of the right hip. Only as a result of this can the right front leg land in front of the right hind leg and go on one track.

This must also happen in the walk and trot. The hippologist Hans von Heydebreck explained this in detail in his book *Die deutsche Dressurprüfung* ("The German Dressage Test"). Straightening in the sense of the Training Scale in the trot and walk is only possible when the horse's forehand—just as in the canter—is brought in front of the hindquarters and the horse is therefore put into minimal flexion and bent to the inside.

Instead, today's equestrian literature often speaks of a seemingly "linear straightening," meaning that the horse should neither be flexed nor bent in the walk and trot. Due to the horse's anatomy (wider hindquarters and narrower forehand), it would be impossible to achieve the previously defined objective of straightening the horse.

Straightening

Conclusion: By "riding in flexion," the horse must be minimally flexed and bent to the inside on the left as well as on the right rein, even in the walk and trot.

Riding in Flexion

In order to fulfill the requirement of straightness in the walk and trot the rider must ride her horse "in flexion" even when on straight lines. The objective when riding in flexion is to improve the straightness of the horse. The horse's outside hind leg should be encouraged to step increasingly between the front hooves. In doing so, the rider must pay special attention to her driving aids: Her outside leg must have a forward-driving and guarding effect and, therefore, indicate the direction of footfall to the horse's outside hind leg. Her inside leg, in contrast, has the function of keeping the horse's inside hind leg on the track.

While this particular horse has an easier time going in flexion on the right rein, the rider must still educate him on the left rein; this can be clearly seen when you look at the rider's inside leg, which is held in a guarding position well behind the girth. In doing so, the rider attempts to prevent the horse's inside hind leg from "escaping."

When there is no outside border on a straight line, the rider must decide where "the inside" is. In this case, he has brought the horse's right shoulder in front of the right hip and has, therefore, decided that "inside" is on the right side.

Practical Tips for Straightening

At the beginning of the young horse's schooling, it is nearly impossible to really sit correctly in the center of the horse. The horse's natural crookedness causes him to shift the rider slightly to one side, which depends on whether the horse is crooked to the right or left side. It is immensely important that the rider does not try to counteract this crookedness. She must not force herself to sit erect and without lateral crookedness, meaning against the horse's crookedness.

As described above, (in most horses) the right side of the rib cage will rise up. At first, an experienced rider must react to the horse's crookedness by carefully following and adjusting to the horse's anatomical reality—that is, the crookedness caused by the bulging rib cage—in a way that the horse almost does not notice, and sit with minimal "crookedness" herself. Even though straightening cannot be improved until relatively late in the horse's education, the experienced rider will still attempt, from the first time she mounts the horse, to positively influence the horse's longitudinal axis and to continuously and carefully counteract the bulging rib cage by riding various turn and shoulder-fore-type exercises.

The Rider Needs a Lot of "Feel"

During the development phase of straightening, the rider can place her inside leg a bit farther back during shoulder-fore-type exercises in order to show the hindquarters "the correct path." She uses her outside leg to prevent the horse's outside hind leg from "escaping." In addition, the rider can use the inside rein to point somewhat toward the inside in supportive fashion in order to bring the inside shoulder in front of the horse's inside hip. Depending on the schooling level, situation, and suppleness of the horse, the rider must decide the level of instructive and supportive aids needed for straightening.

In principle, the rider's *feel* is of essential significance when it comes to straightening the young horse. On the one hand, the rider should "follow" the horse imperceptibly, on the other hand, she must not allow the crooked horse to "assign" a seat position to the rider, which would not be consistent with a straightened horse.

This point highlights how important it is for the inexperienced rider, in turn, to ride an experienced and well-educated schoolmaster.

If the horse was insufficiently schooled and not straightened, the rider would, from the start, be brought into a crooked seat position, or constantly collapse in the hip. Just a few weeks of this type of "seat experience" would suffice for a novice rider to experience this crooked seat as correct and straight! Good-quality, correct riding instruction is impossible under these circumstances.

> **A Matter of Experience**
>
> Once more, we must emphasize the important fact that only an experienced rider with feel is able to straighten a young, naturally crooked horse.

Straightening from the Start?

The experienced rider encounters crookedness from the first time she mounts and, of course, she does not wait until Rhythm, Suppleness, Contact, and Impulsion are developed correctly. She rides curved lines from the beginning of schooling and includes straightening work right from the start. She will try to bring the inside shoulder in front of the inside hip (shoulder-fore-type exercises) during brief phases and ride many turns.

This, once again, highlights the principles of the Training Scale, where each of the six abilities interweave from the beginning, even though not every one of them is fully perfected yet. These abilities do not reach their full potential until many years of schooling are completed.

Therefore, the rider must skillfully utilize the diagonal application of aids to successfully convey the ability of straightening to the young horse.

Only after the horse has learned—by repeated, targeted exercises—to let his outside *hind* leg follow the track of his outside *front* leg, is the rider able to decrease her stronger, instructive leg aids.

At the same time, you must also pay attention to the manner of holding the reins. The goal of schooling should be to lead the straightened horse—whose inside shoulder is in front of the inside hip, and who is (as explained earlier) minimally flexed and bent—with the outside rein. A horse that is not completely straightened is impossible to lead with the outside rein, since he is not yet able to evenly step toward both reins.

It should be your goal to first create even pressure on both reins (by decreasing flexion and encouraging the outside hind leg) and to actively maintain the even bilateral contact with the horse's mouth. Only when this is achieved will it be possible to gradually lead the horse more securely on the outside rein.

Riding in flexion: The horse is flexed in the poll but not bent in the body. You can see the rider's left, outside hand moves forward slightly in order to allow the flexion to the inside.

Exercises for Straightening by Bending

The rider has various possibilities at her disposal to work on straightening the horse. This is called "straightening by bending." This means that riding curved lines and exercises where the horse is in flexion and bend have especially lasting effects on straightening.

Straightening by bending should, therefore, start at the beginning of a riding session or during the first months of the horse's schooling by riding on large, curved lines, and later on tighter curved lines, up to the volte. Initially, this work is done on "one track," meaning on "two-track lines." As complexity increases, you can add the exercises riding in flexion, shoulder-fore, and shoulder-in. All three lessons are important targeted exercises for "straightening by bending." Gradually, you move the horse through these three exercises from two-track lines to three-track lines. None of these three exercises are "true" lateral movements, since in them, the horse is still flexed and bent *against* the direction of movement (in true lateral movement, the horse is flexed and bent *into* the direction of travel), and the hind legs do not yet cross over each other (lateral movement requires crossing). These three exercises are viewed as a link to the work on four-track lines, which are the true lateral movements: renvers, travers, and half-pass.

Every time you ride on curved lines, you should use the operating principle of the three fundamental riding techniques (p. 77) as a guideline for practical work. The diagonal aids that you give on large or small curved lines are always the same. Therefore, we will not explain them here again.

The application of aids for riding the half-pirouette at the walk, shoulder-in, and the lateral movements, is briefly described here:

> **What is Lateral Movement?**
>
> Lateral movements are all those lateral shifts of the horse where he is flexed and bent in the direction of movement, and the front as well as the hind legs cross over with each step.

Half-Pirouette at the Walk

The application of aids is identical to those for turn-on-the-haunches (pirouette at the walk.)

- Prepare the new exercise by means of half-halts.
- Flex the horse in the direction of movement. Shorten the inside rein; the function of the inside rein during the subsequent turn is to give the horse flexion and point him sideways. The outside rein allows the flexion, that is, your hand initially moves forward a bit, the rein then has limiting function.
- The weight aid not only flexes the horse, but also bends him in the direction of movement so that his rib cage slightly lowers, which makes it possible to shift more weight on your inside seat bone.
- The inside leg has the function of supporting the bend and flexion of the horse. It also has a driving function, which is supposed to encourage the horse's inside hind leg to eagerly push off and land in a flat arc. Your inside leg is the predominate leg, while your outside leg has a guarding function: It should limit the bend, prevent the hindquarters from "escaping" and support the horse's outside hind foot in stepping around the inside hind foot.

The lesson is successful when the horse maintains an even degree of flexion and bend during the turn, moves on a small circle with the inside hind foot, and rhythmically pushes off/lands with his foot instead of turning. The horse crosses over with his front legs, but not with his hind legs.

It is required for the horse to maintain all abilities, four beat, suppleness, secure contact, and impulsion, during the exercise.

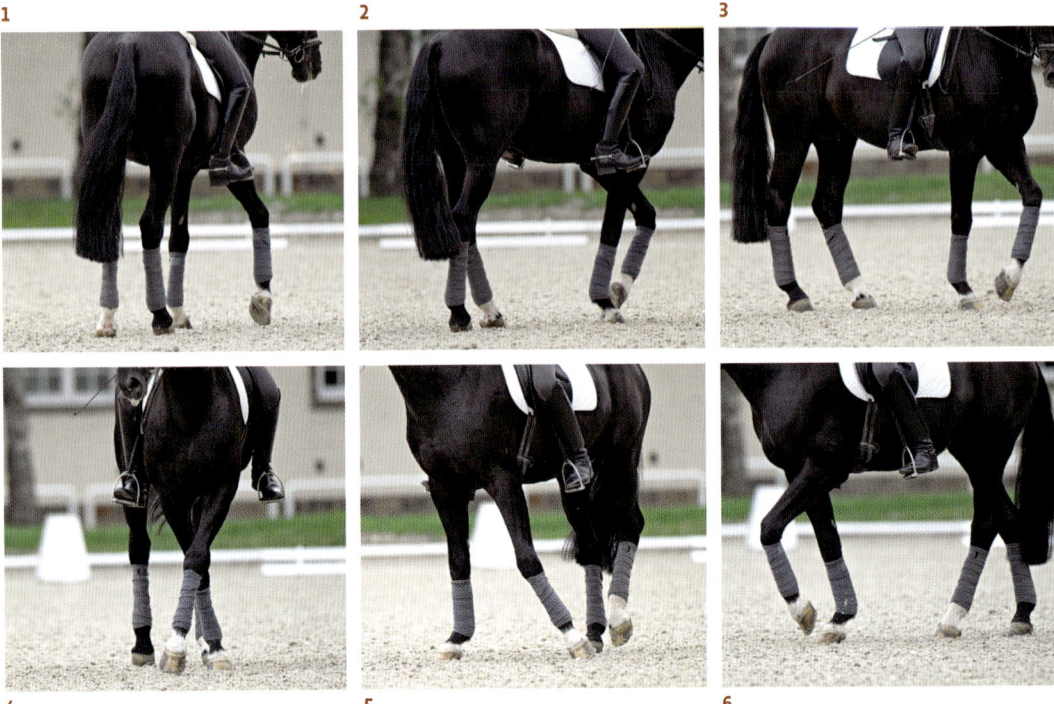

A half-pirouette at the walk to the right, in detail. In the process, the hindquarters move in a circle but do not cross over. In Photo 2, this is not quite successful. A few steps later, in Photo 5, it is done more successfully.

Shoulder-In

- Prepare the lesson by means of half-halts.
- Flex the horse (shorten inside rein; the inside rein gives the horse flexion and points him sideways during the turn). Lengthen the outside rein accordingly (limiting function), and lead the horse's forehand as far to the inside as needed to position the horse's outside front leg in front of the inside hip.
- Shift more weight to the inside.
- The inside leg maintains the bend and encourages the inside hind foot to eagerly push off into the direction of the horse's center of gravity. The outside leg must not be passive. It must prevent the hindquarters from "escaping" and encourage the horse's outside hind leg to eagerly push off.

The lesson is considered successful when the horse's hindquarters stay on the track, while the forehand is led slightly into the arena—meaning far enough to position the outside shoulder of the horse in front of the inside hip of the horse, when viewed from the front. The

Straightening

Shoulder-in-type riding on both reins in the canter. The horse, however, is at too much of an angle in these photos. It would be ideal if you could only see three track lines from the front or the back view—as demonstrated in the small photo.

horse's inside hind leg steps into the direction of the horse's outside front leg, so that you—ideally—only see three legs, when viewed from the front. The front legs cross over, the hind legs do not.

During this exercise, which is considered the ideal preparation for lateral movement, the horse is flexed and bent against the direction of movement. The precondition here is also that the horse maintains all abilities (a clear rhythm, suppleness, secure contact, and impulsion) during the exercise.

The horse's poll must not "tilt to the side." The positive effect on the horse's gait and posture can be felt by the rider: The horse elevates more, meaning he moves in better self-carriage.

The shoulder-in is the important exercise when working on straightening through bending, and is also considered the "mother of all exercises" pertaining to lateral movement. The background: During the shoulder-in, the horse solidifies his ability to straighten, therefore, you simultaneously create all preconditions for collection work. Good collection, in turn, can only be solidified when horse and rider are able to utilize lateral movement.

Lateral Movements

Even though we just determined that lateral movements may be even more useful as they pertain to collection versus straightening, we would like to point out the basic application of aids during lateral movements at this point. The reason is that during daily work, the trainer will not wait until a horse is completely straightened before he begins working with shoulder-in and lateral movements.

He utilizes the exercises when the horse has not yet completely learned all abilities of the Training Scale. The goal is to improve the abilities that were already gained, and to provide the horse with a feel for the movement of subsequent work.

In principle, the application of aids in the lateral movements renvers, travers, and half-pass is the same. The only differences are in the way the exercises are prepared and finished and, furthermore, renvers and travers are usually ridden on the long side, whereas half-pass is ridden on the diagonal through the arena. All lateral movements are ridden on four-track lines. Whether a half-pass is ridden at a flatter or steeper angle primarily depends on the horse's level of schooling, but also on the gymnastic effect the rider is looking to achieve.

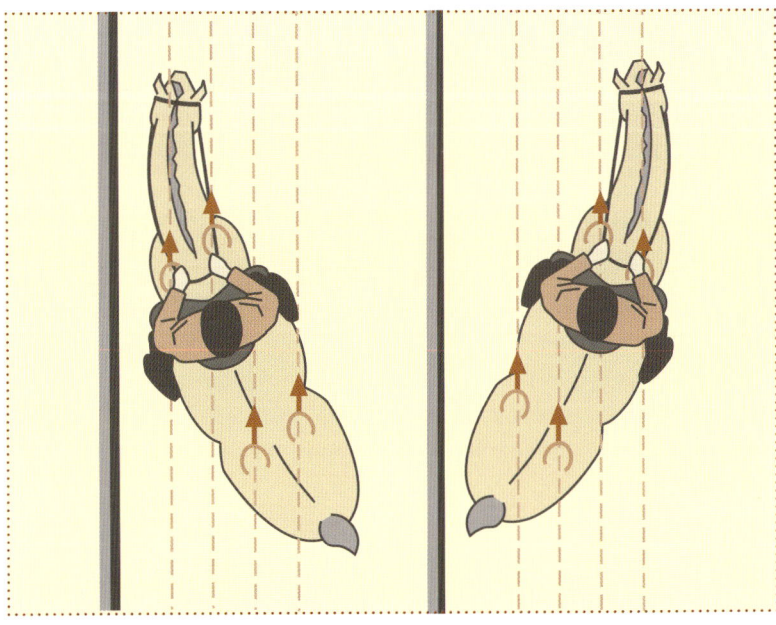

Lateral movements on the long side, on four-track lines. Left: Travers, in which the hindquarters are led into the arena. Right: Renvers, whereby the forehand is led into the arena. In both cases, the horse is flexed and bent into the direction of movement.

Half-Pass

Here is an explanation of the application of aids for the half-pass:
- Prepare the new exercise with half-halts.
- Flex the horse in the direction of movement (shorten inside rein; the function of the inside rein in the subsequent turn is to give the horse flexion and point him sideways). The outside rein allows the flexion (limiting function).
- Guide the forehand in front of the hindquarters, flex the horse into the direction of movement (depending on the direction, your pelvis performs a rolling movement toward the time on the imaginary clock face, either eleven or one o'clock).
- The rider's inside leg maintains the bend and encourages the horse's inside hind foot to step under his body.

The half-pass is an exercise that is extraordinarily suitable for improving collection in the long term. At first, it is ridden at a relatively flat angle. In order to increase the gymnasticizing effect, it may gradually be ridden more steeply up to a zig-zag half-pass, where the changes in direction make the lesson even more valuable.

- The outside leg has a forward and sideways driving function and should prevent the hindquarters from "escaping."
- During the course of the half-pass, both hands can move forward slightly in the direction of movement.

The lesson is considered successful if the horse evenly crosses over with front and hind legs while maintaining a consistent bend. Just as in the previously described exercises, prerequisites for this exercise are the horse staying securely in rhythm, supple, in contact, and maintaining impulsion. The horse goes in half-pass across the diagonal of the arena, and almost parallel to the long side, with the forehand slightly in front of the hindquarters. The hind legs cross up to hock level; the horse seems to "rise up toward" the rider—his self-carriage is improved.

Collection

Meaning of Collection

By working on the abilities Impulsion and Straightening, the rider has created the necessary preconditions for collecting the horse: First, she developed the horse's *pushing power,* an imperative prerequisite for being able to develop the horse's *carrying power* needed for collection.

During the entire further development of the horse it is important to recognize that collection is by no means only useful to dressage horses, but to horses in any kind of discipline.

What Is Collection?

In principle, Collection is defined as the horse's ability to shorten his steps, paces, and strides while maintaining impulsion. It is essential that the horse maintains Suppleness during collection. The chapter about Impulsion explained that the horse must gain an ability to alter the amount of ground covered with each stride. During work on collection this ability gains special significance because the horse shortens his steps, paces, and strides while the arc of his footfalls becomes higher in the process. Furthermore, the collected horse should be "more briefly on the ground and longer in the air." What does this mean? In the gaits

> **Collection**
> After the necessary prerequisites for collection—Impulsion and Straightening—have been established, the horse is able to shorten his steps, paces, and strides while maintaining impulsion.

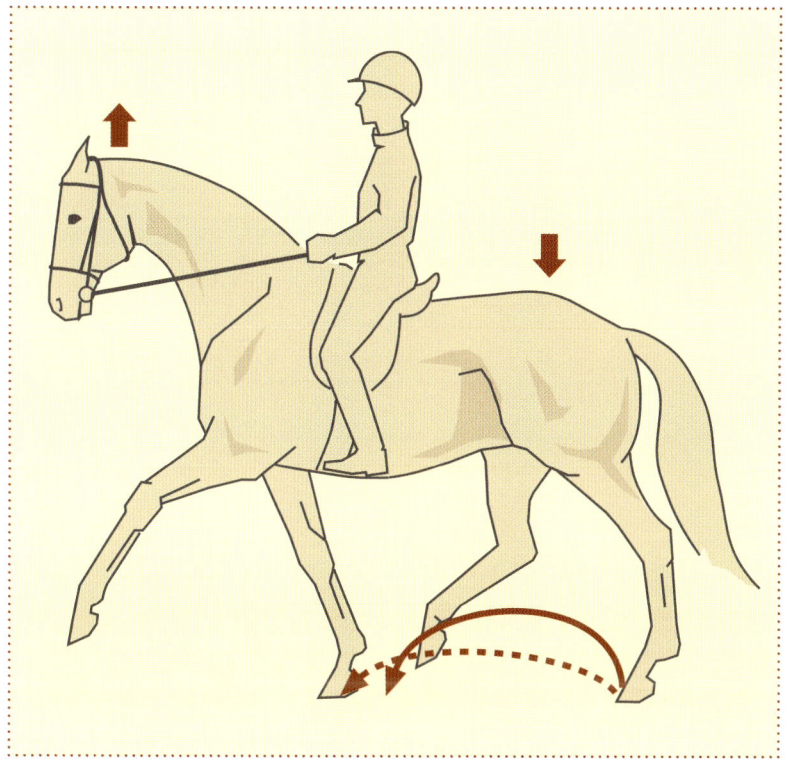

By increasing flexion in the haunches, the horse can "lower" his hind end and elevate his front end. In collection, the arc of the footfall is somewhat higher and shorter, and corresponds with the solid curved line. At a working pace, the arc corresponds with the dotted line, meaning it is flatter and longer. At the same time, the horse's elevation changes to a degree and the horse appears to be "longer".

with impulsion, the horse pushes off the ground quickly and powerfully, and the suspension phases—where no foot touches the ground—become longer at the same time. Only when the horse maintains his impulsion or eagerness in the individual gait, will he have enough *pushing power* to gain the *carrying power* needed for collection.

So far, the focus of developing pushing power has been on the horse's large joints: the hip and the stifle. Now the focus is on the lower joints from the hock down as well. When pushing power was developed, the main goal was to develop the joints' ability to move forward, not their ability to flex, but by doing that, the rider has created the preconditions for flexing the joints, also. The best way to achieve this is to ride lateral movements.

First, use targeted gymnasticizing exercises to achieve identical suppleness in the left and right sides of the horse (this was a major aspect of straightening work).

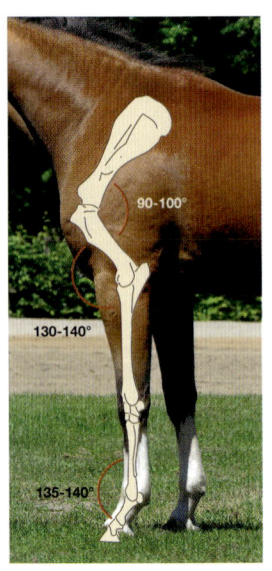

The forehand serves as a support apparatus. Most of the joints of the forehand sit on top of the other in a vertical line, except for angled ones, as shown.

When working on collection, the rider expands the horse's balance by one dimension: The horse gains the ability to flex more in the hip and stifle joints (haunches) and is, therefore, no longer only in lateral balance; the rider creates a shift of balance from the front to the back, meaning from the forehand to the hind end.

It is often said that the rider is "unloading" the horse's forehand by collecting the horse. Some background here: Many riding horses often suffer from tendon, joint, and ligament problems in the forehand. The argument is that the rider's weight places an additional load on the forehand, causing it to wear out prematurely unless she succeeds in riding the horse in collection.

One aspect of this saying is correct: Horses continuously ridden "on the forehand" *are* more likely to suffer from problems in the front limbs. However, measurements have demonstrated that the load taken off the front limbs is hardly greater than 30 kgs, which—in most cases—is not even half the rider's weight. Considering that the total weight of horse and rider is about 700 kgs, this argument seems completely out of proportion.

So it would be more correct to say that the range of motion of the horse's forehand is expanded by more flexion in the haunches, and the horse is, therefore, better able to cushion the riding load overall by flexing these joints, among other things.

There are various indicators of good collection (see page 176). We'll just mention one example here: improved shoulder freedom, which means more flexibility of the front limbs that originate in the shoulder.

Range of movement visibly improves with increased collection: The forehand is able to swing farther and higher, and the horse is better able to bascule over a jump.

Anatomical Background As It Relates to Collection

In principle, the horse's forehand and hindquarters have completely different functions: In nature, the forehand is designed for carrying (support apparatus); in contrast, the hindquarters—with their large joints (hips and stifles)—are responsible for pushing power, and for the horse's movement dynamics (the engine of the horse).

While the joints of the forehand are almost stacked one on top of the other, the horse's haunches—meaning hip and stifle—are angled in such fashion as to allow them to "fold" under a load, reducing their angle and their position toward one another. Through collecting work, the rider strives to achieve a reduction in the angles of these large joints: One of the goals of collection is for the horse to flex more in the haunches.

The result of this increased flexion is that the horse visibly lowers his hindquarters, causing the horse's pelvis to tilt. Due to this tilt, the long back muscle that is attached to the posterior edge of the pelvis on the one end and to the lower cervical vertebrae on the other end causes the horse to increasingly elevate in the neck and poll; it practically "pulls" the horse's forehand and poll upward. This creates the visual impression that the horse now moves in an "uphill" stance.

In riding terminology, there is "relative elevation," which means that the degree of elevation in the horse varies according to the intensity of flexion in the haunches. A young horse that only flexes a little bit is not as elevated as a schooled Grand Prix horse whose haunches can achieve maximum flexion and whose neck and poll are therefore elevated to a much greater degree.

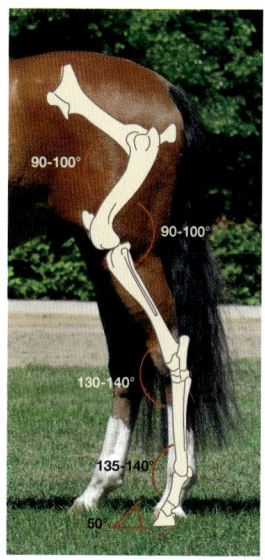

The hind end is the horse's "motor." The angles of the hip and stifle joints, in particular, can change considerably when flexed.

The attempt to elevate young horses too much has nothing to do with reasonable schooling and is always the result of too much hand influence and insufficient shifting of weight to the hind end (known as "absolute elevation").

While the length of stride and, therefore, the arc of the footfall were lengthened during the development of pushing power, now the goal is for the horse to push off the ground more energetically and to step increasingly forward and *upward* at the same time.

Add Variety and Vary the Interplay

Continued schooling of the horse is most successful when you incorporate a variety of different exercises (lessons) and vary the interplay between pushing and carrying power, for example, alternating between lengthening of the frame when riding extensions, and shortening the frame during passage or piaffe.

Dressage tests reflect this working principle of alternating between extension and collection. Recently, there has been a discussion about high-level dressage exercises: Questions were raised about the usefulness of backing up and of the "alternating rein back-forward-rein

The more the horse progresses in his schooling, the better you can discern during the rein-back how the horse flexes his large joints of the hindquarters (left). At the walk, you can also recognize whether the horse is in good self-carriage and how far he steps forward with the hindquarters.

back." There were suggestions to erase the halt from the tests altogether and to abandon alternating between collection and extension in favor of exercise sequences with "audience appeal." So far, however, dressage tests have been reflecting natural gymnasticizing of the horse based on motor science principles. Changing them at will would mean that the sport of dressage is moved far away from classical schooling just for the sake of an artificial, circus-like drill.

Problems When Riding Collected Exercises

The biggest problem when riding in collection is keeping the horse's hindquarters active enough: getting a forward and upward push. Many riders simply ride "slower" by increasing their use of the reins and by doing so, the hindquarters lose their pushing power and impulsion, they "drag" along the ground instead of pushing off energetically and powerfully in a forward and upward direction. Good collection can be easily recognized—especially at the trot: The rear cannon bone and the horse's forearm are parallel to one another (see p. 160).

Many riders "forget" to drive during collection and try to increase their hand influence to achieve collection in the horse. This, however,

can never be done by means of hand influence alone. Instead, the "key" for good collection is the half-halt.

It is hardly possible to ride half-halts with more refinement than when in collection where subtlety is of the essence: The rider must rely more strongly on using weight aids without blocking her pelvis in the process. This possible blockage would translate into a bumping movement that would have a negative effect on the horse's back and disturb the flow of his movement.

During collecting exercises, the rider should let her pelvis "tilt" to the back. Don't get stuck in this position; allow it forward again in accordance with the trot or canter movement. Imagine the face of a

During collection, the horse is supposed to flex his haunches, meaning his hip and stifle joints. This, in turn, has an effect on all other joints below the stifle, down to the fetlock joints, which also have increased flexion.

The key to good collection is the half-halt.

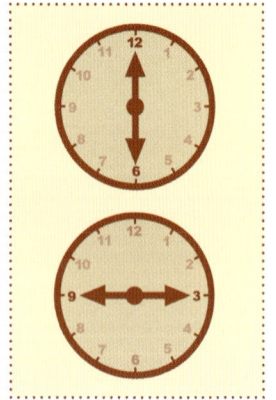

clock: The pelvis always moves from a center position of the pelvis (slightly tilted forward) back to the 6 and then back into the center. As previously explained, this backward movement of the pelvis can be achieved and practiced by "tucking in the belly button," even when riding collecting exercises. Prerequisites, however, are flexibility in the pelvis from front to back (on a clock, from 12 to 6), and from right to left (on a clock, from 3 to 9). You can support the increased application of weight aids by a rhythmic, brief contraction of the abdominal muscles in unison with the horse's rhythm and gait.

Since the human abdominal musculature has a tendency to become weak, most people have problems when it comes to finding the right way to use it. For this reason, riders should learn to strengthen and utilize their abdominal muscles.

The following exercises can be performed in static or slowly dynamic fashion. When performing the exercise in a static fashion, first, hold the muscle tension for 8–10 seconds after completing the exercise. Continue to breathe during this time. You can now extend this time or hold the tension for 8–10 seconds, repeatedly. In between repetitions, you should take a break of 8–10 seconds.

The slow dynamic sequences should be repeated 8–12 times (a set). When executing several sets in succession, take a break of 10–15 seconds between sets. You should start with an appropriate number of repetitions, according to your personal fitness level.

Strengthening Abdominal Muscles

Starting Position: Lie on your back, bend knee and hip joints to form a right angle, cross your arms in front of the upper body.
Execution: Slowly lift the upper body; your head remains an extension of your body (do not press the chin onto the chest).

Starting Position: Lie on your back with knees bent, stretch the arms forward—see page 21.
Execution: Slowly lift the upper body and stretch the arms forward past the legs.

Starting Position: Lie on your back, bend knee and hip joints to form a right angle; hold lower legs up or place them on a chair.

Execution: Lift your upper body; raise the left shoulder off the ground and reach with both hands past the right thigh—see page 21.

Mobilization of the Back
Starting Position: Lie on your back, bend knee and hip joints to form a right angle, slightly open your legs.
Execution: Alternately place your legs on the ground to the right, then to the left side.

Extensions
In principle, it is possible to check the level of collection of a horse from his extensions. Incidentally, this is also a reason why dressage tests require the rider to frequently alternate collected and extended tempi.

One cannot just ask the horse for collection. It has to be developed through a meaningful, systematic "series of exercises," building from elementary to advanced.

One Example: In principle, schooling should always start at a working gait. This is also the gait used for the suppling phase (elementary). A meaningful step up is to then lengthen the steps in the trot, or to expand the canter strides. From there, you develop beginning collection (it is gradually getting more complex). Based upon beginning collection, you consequently develop the medium trot or medium canter. The difference between lengthening steps and expanding strides: When *expanding* strides, you *gradually* enlarge the frame and ground coverage; slowing down also takes several strides. When riding medium trot or medium canter, however, the lengthened stride can be shown immediately, without going by degrees.

From medium trot or medium canter you develop a better-quality collection. Once you have this, you can develop the extended gaits.

Conclusion: The Effects of Collection
The effects of high-quality collection are manifold:
- When the horse flexes the haunches, his "support area" becomes smaller. This makes it easier to ride smaller turns: The horse can nearly "turn on a dime," so to speak. This—on the one hand—could mean a pirouette in dressage, or—on the other hand—the rapid, extremely tight turns of show jumpers on the jump-off course.
- Due to the increased flexion of the haunches, the forehand gains freedom of movement. The horse is able to move his front legs more freely—with the movement coming from the shoulders—and to take shorter steps while swinging farther forward and upward. For the show jumper, the collection provides the advantage of being able to pull up his front limbs more evenly and at a tighter angle over the jump. In a dressage horse, it serves to make a relatively upright shoulder visually more "sloped."
- Once pushing power and carrying power are developed to a great extent, there is a visible impact on the gaits with impulsion. The horse seems more elastic; it seems as if he could push off and land with more suppleness. In many horses that are still in the process of being schooled, you can hear loudly and clearly every time the horse's foot lands on the ground, almost as if the horse is "falling" from one foot to the other. With increasing schooling levels, the horse's gait becomes more "springy" and, therefore, less audible. The dressage horse pushes off with elastically flexed joints and lands more softly. The show jumper shows more bascule and is able to land more elastically after the jump. This interplay between pushing power and carrying power is also called the development of "springiness," or an expression of more "cadence."
- The foundation for positive tension that was created toward the end of basic schooling (see Contact on p. 140) is now increasingly refined and perfected. As the schooling progresses, the rider must, time and

again, check whether the basic preconditions, Rhythm, Suppleness, and Contact are firmly established, before you develop pushing power and carrying power.
- All previously developed abilities continue to improve with collection. Riding comfort increases, application of aids can be reduced to a minimum, and contact stays steady but light. Overall, the process of riding is substantially "easier" for rider and horse.

> **What is Cadence?**
> The interaction of the horse's pushing power and carrying power is called the development of "springiness." The way the horse's foot pushes off and lands with more elasticity and energy makes the horse appear larger and more elegant, among other things. This is the horse moving with cadence.

> **At a Glance**
> - The explanation of all six abilities of the Training Scale provides substantiation for the gymnasticizing principles that provide the backdrop for the Training Scale.
> - Depending on the goals and requirements of rider and horse, you are able to use the Training Scale to start a conversation with your horse through meaningful, systematic steps.
> - When training your horse, you must fulfill many of the biomechanical requirements we've discussed in order to begin a conversation.
> - Only from an already schooled horse can the beginner rider learn the feel for movement that is needed for conversation.
> - When these principles are not followed, you can no longer speak of schooling the horse; in this case, the horse is being "drilled."

Bibliography

Autorenliste 1: u. a. Engelke/Hlatky 2007, Hirtz/Hummel 2003, Hirtz/Nüske 1997, Hirtz/Hotz/Ludwig 2000, Heuer 1997, Kunert 2009, Lange 2005, Lange 2010, Loosch 1999, Scheid/Prohl 2001, 2003, Schnabel/Harre /Borde 1997, Weineck 2007

Autorenliste 2: u. a. Hirtz/Nüske 1997, Hirtz/Hotz/Ludwig 2000, Meyners 2009, Scheid/Prohl 2001, 2003, Weineck 2007

Autorenliste 3: u. a. Bertram/Laube 2008, Hirtz/Hotz/Ludwig 2000, Hirtz/Nüske 1997, Kirchner/Pöhlmann 2005, Schöllhorn/Michelbrink/Grzybowsky 2007

Ayres, A.J./Robins, J.: Bausteine der kindlichen Entwicklung. Die Bedeutung der Integration der Sinne für die Entwicklung des Kindes. Berlin 1998

Beckmann, H./Schöllhorn, W.: Differenzielles Lernen im Kugelstoßen. In: Leistungssport 36 (2006) 4, S. 44 – 50

Beckmann, H./Gotzes, D.: Differenzielles Lehren und Lernen in der Leichtathletik. In: Sportunterricht 58 (2009) 2, S. 46 – 50

Beckmann, H./Wastl, P.: Perspektiven für die Leichtathletik – Nachwuchsarbeit und Differenzielles Lehren und Lernen. Hamburg 2009

Bertram, A.M./Laube, W.: Sensomotorische Koordination. Gleichgewichtstraining mit dem Kreisel. Stuttgart/New York 2008

Bürger, U./Zietschmann, O.: Der Reiter formt das Pferd. Reprint von 1939, Warendorf 2007

Deutsche Reiterliche Vereinigung (Hg.): Richtlinien für Reiten und Fahren, Band 1, Warendorf 2005

Deutsche Reiterliche Vereinigung (Hg.): Richtlinien für Reiten und Fahren, Band 2, Warendorf 2001

Engelke, K./Hlatky, M.: Bewegung beginnt im Kopf. Koordination macht´s perfekt. Wien 2007

Ennenbach, W.: Bild und Mitbewegung. Köln 1989

Göhner, U.: Einführung in die Bewegungslehre. Band 1, Reinbek 1992; Band 2, 1999

Gröben, B./Maurus, P.: Bewegungsanweisungen – Hilfe oder Hindernis beim Erlernen sportlicher Bewegungen? In: Barb, H./Laging, R. (Hg.) Bewegungslernen in Erziehung und Bildung. Hamburg 1999, S. 103 – 106

HDV 12: Reitvorschrift vom 29. Juni 1912, Berlin 1912

Hirtz, P./Hummel, A.: Motorisches Lernen im Sportunterricht. In: Mechling, H./Munzert, J. (Hg.) Handbuch Bewegungswissenschaft - Bewegungslehre. Schorndorf 2003

Hirtz, P./Nüske, F. (Hg.): Bewegungskoordination und sportliche Leistung integrativ betrachtet. Hamburg 1997

Hirtz, P./Hotz, O./Ludewig, G.: Bewegungskompetenzen. Gleichgewicht. Schorndorf 2000

Heuer, H.: Strukturelle Rahmenbedingungen der Koordination. In: Loosch, E./Tamme, M. (Hg.) Motorik – Struktur und Funktion. Hamburg 1997, S. 39 – 52

Jasper, B.M.: Koordination und Gehirnjogging. Aachen 2003

Kirchner, G./Pöhlmann, R.: Lehrbuch der Sportmotorik. Kassel 2005 (Kap. 4, psychomotorische-koordinative Fähigkeiten)

Kolb, M.: Methodische Prinzipien zur Entwicklung der Körperwahrnehmung. In: Schierz, M./Hummel, A./Balz, E. (Hg.) Sportpädagogik. Orientierungen, Leitideen, Konzepte. St. Augustin 1994, S. 239 – 260

Kosel, A.: Schulung der Bewegungskoordination. Schonrdorf 2005, 7. Aufl.

Kunert, Ch.: Koordination und Gleichgewicht. Wiebelsheim 2009

Lange, H.: Facetten qualitativen Bewegungslernens. Immenhausen bei Kassel 2005

Lange, H.: Koordinationslernen – Pädagogische Begründung eines unterrichtspraktischen Modells: In: Sportpraxis 51 (2010) Sonderheft, S. 4 – 9

Loosch, E.: Allgemeine Bewegungslehre. Wiebelsheim 1999

Meinel, K./Schnabel, G.: Bewegungslehre – Sportmotorik. Berlin 2007, 11. Aufl.

Meyners, E.: Reiten – ein Dialog zwischen Mensch und Pferd. In: Meyners, E. Lehren und Lernen im Reitsport. Lüneburg 2002, 2. Aufl., S. 30 – 46

Meyners, E.: Bewegungsgefühl für Reiter. Langwedel-Völkersen 2008 (DVD)

Meyners, E.: Übungsprogramm im Sattel. Langwedel-Völkersen 2009 (DVD)

Meyners, E. : Der Sitz beim Stellen und Biegen. In: Dressurstudien 5 (2009 – 2) 3, 62 – 68

Meyners, E.: Integrative Bewegungslehre im Reiten – das Bemühen um eine ganzheitliche Sichtweise von Bewegung. In: Dressurstudien 2010

Neumaier, A.: Koordinatives Anforderungsprofil und Koordinationstraining. Grundlagen – Analyse – Methodik. Köln 1999

Oliver, N.: Zur Fertigkeitsspezifik der Gleichgewichtsregulation. In: Loosch, E./Tamme, M. (Hg.) a. a. O., S. 72 – 75

Römer, J./Schöllhorn, W./Jaiter, Th./Preiss, R.: Differenzielles Lernen im Volleyball. In: Sportunterricht 58 (2009) 2, S. 41 – 45

Roth, K.: Wie verbessert man die koordinativen Fähigkeiten? In: Bielefelder Sportpädagogen (Hg.) Methoden im Sportunterricht. Schorndorf 1998, 3. Aufl. , S. 85 – 102

Roth, K./Willimczik, K.: Bewegungswissenschaft. Reinbek 1999

Scheid, V./Prohl, R.: Bewegungslehre. Wiebelsheim 2001, 6. Aufl.

Scheid, V./Prohl, R.: Trainingslehre. Wiebelsheim 2003, 8. Aufl.

Schinauer, Th.: Zielbewegungskoordination ganzheitlich betrachtet. In: Loosch, E./Tamme, M. (Hg.) a. a. O., S. 61 – 71

Schnabel, G./Harre, D./Borde, A. (Hg.): Trainingswissenschaft. Leistung – Training – Wettkampf. Berlin 1997, 2. Aufl.

Schöllhorn, W.: Individualität – ein vernachlässigter Parameter? In: Leistungssport 29 (1999) 2, S. 4 – 12

Schöllhorn, W.: Eine Sprint- und Laufschule. Aachen 2003

Schöllhorn, W./Sechelmann, M./Trockel, M./Westers, R.: Nie das Richtige trainieren, um richtig zu lernen. In: Leistungssport 34 (2004) 5, S. 13 – 17

Schöllhorn, W.: Differenzielles Lehren und Lernen von Bewegung – Durch veränderte Annahmen zu neuen Konsequenzen. In: Gabler, H./Göhner, U./Schiebl, F. (Hg.) Zur Vernetzung von Forschung und Lehre in Biomechanik, Sportmotorik und Trainingswissenschaft. Hamburg 2005, S. 125 – 136

Schöllhorn, W.: Schnelligkeitstraining. DVD. Weikersheim 2006

Schöllhorn; W./Michelbrink, M./Grzybowsky, C.: Gleichgewichtstraining (DVD). Weikersheim 2007

Schöllhorn; W./Michelbrink, M./Grzybowsky, C.: Grundlagen des differenziellen Lernens beim alpinen Skifahren. In: Leistungssport 37 (2007) 3, S. 36 – 41; Leistungssport 37 (2007) 4, S. 58 – 62

Schöllhorn, W./Humpert, V./Oelenberg, M./Michelbrink, M./Beckmann, H.: Differenzielles und Mentales Training im Tennis. In: Leistungssport 38 (2008) 6, S. 10 – 14 Sportunterricht Schwerpunktheft: Differenzielles Lernen 58 (2009) 2

Schöllhorn, W./Beckmann, H./Janssen, D./Michelbrink, M.: Differenzielles Lehren und Lernen im Sport. In: Sportunterricht 58 (2009) 2, S. 36 – 40

Steinbrecht, Gustav: Das Gymnasium des Pferdes. Postdam 1892

Tamboer, J.: Sich-Bewegen – ein Dialog zwischen Mensch und Welt. In: Sportpädagogik 3 (1979) 2, S. 60 – 65

Tholey, P.: Prinzipien des Lehrens und Lernens sportlicher Handlungen aus gestalttheoretischer Sicht. In: Janssen, J.P./Schlicht, W./Strang, H. (Hg.) Handlungskontrolle und soziale Prozesse im Sport. Köln 1987

Trebels, A. H.: Das dialogische Bewegungskonzept. Eine pädagogische Auslegung. In: Sportunterricht 41 (1992) 1, S. 20 – 29

Trebels, A. H.: Bewegung sehen und beurteilen. In: Sportpädagogik 14 (1990) 1, S. 12 – 20

Volger, B.: Lehren von Bewegungen. Ahrensburg 1990

von Heydebreck, H.: Die deutsche Dressurprüfung, Singhofen, 3. Aufl. 1988

Weineck, J.: Optimales Training. Erlangen 2007, 15. Aufl.

Index

Page numbers in *italics* indicate illustrations.

Abdominal muscles, 92, 134–35, 182–83
Ability, 17–18
Absolute elevation, 179
Advanced development phase
 collection, 176–185
 impulsion, 148–161
 overview, 145–47
 straightness, 161–176
Aids. *See also* Driving aids; Leg aids; Rein aids
 vs. auxiliary means, 58
 bilateral, 45–46, 50, 88
 coordination of, 19, 58–59, *59*, 84, 92, 141, 156
 diagonal, 82, 87–92, 169
 effects of, 28–29, 74
 in half-halts, 94–95, 97–98
 independent, 59, 61
 overview, 42–44, *43*
 restraining, 43, 141, 156
 timing of, 127–133
 unilateral, 48–49, *48*, 50, 88
 weight as, 43–49, *43–45*, 54–55
Arena figures, *78*
Arm position, 56–57, *57*
Army Regulations of 1912, 1–3
Attention, direction of, 122

Back
 of horse, *11*, *12*, 89–90, *90*, 138–39
 of rider, 133–35, 154–55, 183
Balance, of horse, 25–26, 27, 79, 157–58
Balance, of rider
 biomechanics of, 19–20, 22
 coordination of aids and, 61
 exercises for, 30–35, *30–34*
 factors in, 24–27, *26*
 in rider's training scale, 72–73
 types of, 23
Balimo Chairs, 46–47, *46–47*, 83
Barrel, of horse, 86–87
Belly, tucking of, 154–55
Bending
 in developing straightness, 169–171
 gymnasticizing role, 77–81
 rider exercises for, 92–93
 technique of, 86–92, *86–87*
Biomechanics, 17–19, 23

Cadence, 184–85
Canter
 impulsion in, 160–61
 rhythm of, 132–33, *132*
 rider influence on, *60*, 109
 transitions, *48*, 160–61
Carrying power, 74, 108–9, 176, 179, 184–85
Chewing, by horse, 137
Circles, *78*, *86*
Collection
 anatomy and, 178–79, *181*
 effects of, 184–85
 extended gaits and, 183–84
 half-halts in, 94
 impulsion and, 184
 meaning of, 176–78, *177*
 rider influence on, 180–82
Communication, 112–123. *See also* Aids; Conversational-movement
Conditioning
 of horse, 145–47
 of rider, 9, 17, *17*, 20–22, *21*
Conformation, 77–79
Contact, 125, 140–42, *141–42*
Contrasting experiences, *120*, *121*
Conversational-movement, viii–ix, 10–15, 74
Cool-down, 70–71, *128*, *129*
Coordination
 of horse, 145–47
 of rider, 11, 17, *17*, 24, 64–65

Core muscles, 92, 134–35, 182–83
Crookedness, of horse, 77, 79, 82, 87, 109, 163–65, 168–69. *See also* Straightness
Cross-coordination, 23, 41–42, 64, 93, *93*, 98–99
Curved lines. *See* Bending

Direction of travel, 44, *78*, 81, 94, 108, 139
Driving aids. *See also* Leg aids
 function of, 127, 151–54, 167, *168*
 in gaits, 130, 131–32, 157, 159
 interplay with restraining, 141, 156
 overview, 43, 49–54, *53–54*

Endurance. *See* Conditioning
Energy, in walk, 155–59
Energy-oriented ability, 17–18, *17*
Extended gaits, *150*, 183–84
Eyes, or rider, 35–36

Familiarization phase
 contact, 140–42
 overview, 125
 rhythm, 125–133
 suppleness, 135–39
Feel
 in evaluating riding, 13–14
 in half-halts, 94–97
 instructional challenges, 112–13, 116, 117–123
 refinement of, *14*, 127–130, 139, 151, 164–66, 168–69
Fitness. *See* Conditioning
Flexion
 gymnasticizing role, 77–81
 straightness and, 166, *168*, *170*
 technique of, 81–84, *81–82*
Foot position, 53–54, *53*, 152
Forehand
 collection and, 178–79, *178*

in impulsion, 150
turns on, 109, *109*
Frame, of horse, 29, 44, *54*, 88–92
Freedom from constraint, 135
Functional riding instruction
    communication in, 112–123
    goals in, 105, 106, 110
    overview, 101–3
    planning for, 103–6, 110
    riding theory in, 107–11
    task-orientation in, 106, 110–11, 116–123

Gaits, 108–9, 155–161. *See also specific gaits*
German National Equestrian Federation, 1–2
Giving, of reins, 137–38, *138*, 139, *140*
Gluteal muscles, 133–34
Guarding leg, 51–52, 88, 91, 168
Gymnasticizing principles, 77–81

Half-halts
    function of, 77–81, 181–82
    technique of, 94–98
Half-pass, 174, 175–76, *175*
Half-pirouette, in walk, 79, 109, *142*, 159, 171, *172*
Halts and halting, 80
Hand position, 57–58, 83–84
Harmony, 15
Haunches, turns on, 109. *See also* Hindquarters
Head
    of horse, 130, 137
    of rider, 35–36, *35–36*, 85, 156
Hindquarters
    collection and, 177–79, *179*
    in impulsion, 150–51
Hock joints, 150–51, 177–79

Imagery. *See* Visual learning
Impulsion
    anatomy and, 149–151
    collection role, 176–77, 184

decreasing, 154–55, *154*
development of, 147, 148–49, 151–54
in gaits, 155–161
overview, 148–49
rider influence on, 97, 151, 153–54
Influence, 24, 25–26, 27
Information-oriented ability, 17–18, *17*
Inside leg
    bending role, 90
    in diagonal aids, 82, 87–92, 169
Instructors, 15, *75*, 106, 116. *See also* Functional riding instruction
Intention, 118–19

Joint mobility, 65–66, *181*

Knee joint flexibility, 92

Language, learning through, 115–16, 117–123
Lateral balance, 77–79
Lateral movements, 170–71, 174–78
Learning styles, 112–16
Leg aids
    exercises for, 38, *38*, 40–42, *41–42*, 54–55, *55*
    function of, 51, 152
    overview, 49–54, *49*, *51–53*
    reins/weight and, 43–44, *43*, 54–55
Leg-yielding, 89, 139, *140*
Lengthening, of stride, *150*, 159–160
Lessons. *See* Functional riding instruction
Longitudinal bend, 89–90

Mental attitude, 66, 69–71
Mouth, of horse, 137
Movements
    of horse, 7–9, 24, 147
    of rider, 118–120

"Nagging," with aids, 49, 157
Natural movements, 7–8
Neck
    of horse, 130, 137–38
    of rider, 35–36, *35–36*, 72, 156

Passage, 7–9
Pelvic flexibility. *See also* Pelvis, of rider
    exercises for, 38, *38–39*, 46–47, *46–47*, 85, *85*
    function of, 82–85, 91, 152–53, 156, *157*, 181–82
    horse's back and, *11*, 12
    rider's back and, 133–35
Pelvis, of horse, 150–51, 177–79
Pelvis, of rider, 44–45, 48, *48*, 72, 90–91, *91*, 95–96, 156. *See also* Pelvic flexibility
Perception, instruction and, 117–123
"Pestering," with aids, 49, 157
Physical condition. *See* Conditioning
Piaffe, 7–9
Position, of rider, 33, 40–42, *41–42*. *See also* Aids
Positive tension, 142–43, 184–85
Posture. *See* Frame, of horse
Praise, 45, 137
Preparation. *See* Warm-up
Principles of Riding and Driving, 1–2, 8–9
Proprioception, 73–74, 97
Pushing power, 163, 177–78, 180–82, 184–85

Recovery phase, 70–71, *128*, 129
Rein aids. *See also* Contact
    function of, *56–57*, 92, 130, *158*, 169
    "giving away" of, 137–38, *138*, 139, *140*
    legs/weight and, 43–44, *43*, 54–55
    refinement of, 84, 119–120
    upper body position and, 153–54, *154*

Rein-back, *180*
Relative elevation, 179
Relaxation. *See* Suppleness
Renvers, 174, *174*
Rhythm
  balance factors, 24–27
  in familiarization phase, 125–133
  regulation of, 126–28, 146
  rider influence on, 19–20, 27, 28–29, 72–73
Rib cage, of horse, 86–87, 89–90
Riding
  as conversation, 10–15
  evaluation of, 13–14
  instruction in (*see* Functional riding instruction)
Riding theory, 8–9, 107–11

Sacroiliac joint, of rider, 39, *39*, 135, *135*, 152–53, 156
Schooling. *See* Training
Seat
  effective use of, 22, 32, 154–56
  exercises for, 33–34, *33*
Serpentines, *78*, 103–5
Shape. *See* Frame, of horse
Shortening, of stride, 159–160, *160*, 176
Shoulder
  of horse, 178, 184
  of rider, 37, *38*, 40–42, *40–41*, 84–85, *85*, 92
Shoulder-fore exercises, 168
Shoulder-in, *83*, 172–73, *173*
6-Point Program exercises, 35–45
Skill, 19
Soundness, 77, 79
Speed, 94, 146
Spurs, 58

Stiffness, of rider, 33, 72. *See also* Suppleness
Stifle joints, 150–51, 177, 178–79
Stirrups, 32, 50, 152, 157
Straightness
  benefits of, 161–64, *162*, *165*
  development of, 168, 170–76
  gymnasticizing for, 77–79, *142*
Strength. *See* Conditioning
Stretching exercises, 20–22, *21*
Stride length, *108*, 148–49, 159–160, *160*, 176
Suppleness
  of horse, 136–39, *136*, 146
  of rider, *18*, 72, 74, 139 (*see also* Pelvic flexibility)
Suspension phase, *28*, 96, 109, 128, *131*, *132*, 148–49, 155–56

Tail, as indicator of suppleness, 139, *139*
Task-oriented riding instruction, 106, 110–11, 116–123
Tempo, 44, 108
Three-dimensional flexibility, 133–35, 152–53
Tracking up, 164
Training
  traditions of, 1–4
  variety in, 179–180
Training Scale. *See also specific elements*
  advanced development phase, 145–47
  familiarization phase, 125
  goals of, 4
  in lesson planning, 101
  overview, 2–3, 5–9, 169
  for riders, 71–75
Transitions
  benefits of, *107*, 139, 158–161

downward, 154–55
within gaits, 158–59
rider pelvis and, 153–54
Travers, *59*, *79*, 174, *174*
Trot
  rhythm of, 130–32, *131*
  rider influence on, *60*, 109, *131*, 132
  transitions and, 159–160, *160*
Trust, 72
Turns
  benefits, 109 (*see also* Bending)
  on forehand/haunches, 109, *109*

"Uphill" balance, 178–79
Upper body, 36–37, *36–37*, 45, 72, 153–54

Visual learning, 112, 114, 118, 120
Voice, 58

Walk
  balance in, *10*
  half-pirouette in, *79*, 109, *142*, 159, 171, *172*
  impulsion and, 155–59
  rhythm of, *28*, 108–9, 128–130, *128*
  transitions within, 158–59
Warm-up
  benefits of, 63–66, 125, 145
  guidelines for, 67–71, *69–70*
Weight aids, 43–49, *43–45*, 54–55
Whips, 58
Working gaits, 7, 105, *108*, 109, 177, 183
Wrist flexibility, 84, *85*